COPING WITH CONTROL AND MANIPULATION

COPING WITH CONTROL AND MANIPULATION

Making the Difference Between Being a Target and Becoming a Victim

Vera Sonja Maass

PRAEGER

AN IMPRINT OF ABC-CLIO, LLC
Santa Barbara, California • Denver, Colorado • Oxford, England

Library of Congress Cataloging-in-Publication Data

Maass, Vera Sonja.
 Coping with control and manipulation : making the difference between being a target and becoming a victim / Vera Sonja Maass.
  p. cm.
 Includes bibliographical references and index.
 ISBN 978-0-313-38577-3 (hbk. : alk. paper)—ISBN 978-0-313-38578-0 (ebook)
1. Manipulative behavior. 2. Control (Psychology) 3. Interpersonal relations.
I. Title.
 BF632.5.M32   2010
 158.2—dc22   2010011868

ISBN: 978-0-313-38577-3
EISBN: 978-0-313-38578-0

14 13 12 11 10   1 2 3 4 5

This book is also available on the World Wide Web as an eBook.
Visit www.abc-clio.com for details.

ABC-CLIO, LLC
130 Cremona Drive, P.O. Box 1911
Santa Barbara, California 93116-1911

This book is printed on acid-free paper ∞

Manufactured in the United States of America

Contents

Preface   ix

Acknowledgments   xi

1. The Multifaceted Nature of Control   1
   Controlling the Environment as Means of Controlling Others   3
   Expectations and Their Controlling Effects   3
   The Deception-Expectation Alliance   8
   Deception in the Marketplace   9
   Theoretical Views of Control Behaviors   10
   Control Techniques   11
   Control on a Larger Scale: Groups   12
   Control within the Self   15

2. Origins and Development of Control Attempts   17
   Early Practice of Controlling Behaviors   17
   Laying the Foundations for Personality Patterns   18
   Parents' Control Strategies   20
   Learning Mastery and Constraint   21
   Personality Patterns and Control   23

Attachment Styles and Control   24
Strivings for Perfection and Control   27
The Control Obsession   28
Fear as Motivator in Control Strivings   29
Competition and the Fear of Failure   30
The Persistent Personality and Control   31
A Narrow Escape   32

3. **A Menu of Control Techniques**   35
Interaction Rituals: Systems of Society-Sanctioned Control   35
Language and Speech Patterns as Control Techniques   37
Temper Tantrums, Emotional Blackmail   41
Ingratiating Behaviors   44
The Goals behind Control Techniques   47
Discovering the Goals in Applied Control Techniques   50
Misguided Control Techniques   52

4. **Contestants in the Control Dance**   55
Control Tactics from Those We Know   56
Controlling Friends   57
Beliefs and Their Role in Control Situations   59
Control in Intimate Relationships   60
Emotional State and Physically Violent Control   65
Lady Macbeth, Cleopatra, and the Modern Women   67
It Takes Two to Tango   69
The Approach–Avoidance Dance   70
Control as Relationship Glue   71

5. **Players in the World of Work and Business**   75
When Business Is Combat, It Pays to Have an Army   76
Competitive Values and Control in Business   78
Keeping the Prospective Customer on a Tight Leash   79
Paychecks Demanding Loyalty   81
Controlling with Brand Names   83
Opposing Goals and Conflicting Values in Family Enterprises   86
Competition—All in the Family   88
Guessing and Mind Reading in the Pursuit of Business Advantages   89

6. **Marketing for Control**   93
Propaganda   94
Persuasion   96
Psychological Principles as a Basis for Control   97
Techniques of Persuasion   98
The Indirect Technique of Self-Persuasion   102
Packaging   103

Image Packaging and Targets' Expectations 104
The Use of Language 106
The Suggestive Function of Emotional Language 106
Controlling the Transmission of Public Information 107
Tips for Control 108

7. **Control within the Self** 111
Self-Regulation 111
Breakdown of Self-Regulation 112
Anger, Jealousy, and Envy: Emotions Leading to Self-Regulation
  Breakdowns 114
Internal Struggle for Control: Obsessions, Compulsions,
  Superstitions 117
Exaggerated Need for Order 120
Self-Management Activities 124
Self-Managing Charisma 124
Self-Help Books and Self-Control 125
Self-Regulatory System Repair 126
Self-Discipline from Beginning to End 127

8. Re-Creating One's Self 129
Taking Control of Your Life Workshop—An Arena for
  Self-Restructuring 131
Me and My Shadow—An Example of Self-Restructuring 135

References 149

Index 155

Preface

The idea for this book came from conducting personal growth workshops for the general public with the title "Taking Control of Your Life"—a topic that has attracted people for a long time. Male and female participants came from a variety of backgrounds, with one characteristic in common: they all viewed themselves as victims of others' pursuits of control. In their own minds, they were casualties, caught in the net of the great control struggles of those around them. Only a few of them recognized that at times they themselves had exerted control over others, but compared with the control pursuits directed at them, their own attempts seemed minimal. And, of course, many of the participants knew about control "freaks" they had encountered, but very few admitted to possessing such characteristics themselves.

During the group experiences, participants—by observing others—realized that their own attempts to influence people in their environment had been more numerous than they ever admitted to themselves or others. However, rather than point the finger at participants engaged in controlling behaviors, the group members came to recognize it as a positive sign, reflecting that they had not been as helpless as they believed they were.

As members of the group, participants learned to observe and recognize signals that those who were attempting to control them unwittingly emitted. They also learned to develop efficient and effective behavioral responses to those power struggles and control attempts. Connecting the participants' experiences to theoretical frameworks and linking them to relevant research findings greatly facilitated the learning process and eventually led to the notion of making it a major part of this book. Although the group experience provided the major impetus for the book, personal accounts from clients and from people in the community at large completed the background.

The book's purpose is to dispel the myths of helplessness and the intimidating aspects associated with the use of control. While emphasizing the resilience of intended target persons, the book offers readers encouragement to explore their options and to refuse becoming enabling victims in the service of controllers and power holders in their environment.

The individuals, whose situations have been discussed in this book—the group members, individual clients, and volunteers from the community—deserve appreciation for their disclosures as well as the respect for their privacy. Therefore, for reasons of confidentiality, all names have been changed and some of the persons' circumstances have been disguised. This book gives them all a voice with which to encourage others.

Acknowledgments

To all the individuals who agreed to share their stories, I give my appreciation. Their willingness and enthusiasm was gratifying; although they remain nameless to protect their privacy, they all deserve my thanks.

Special thanks are extended to Debbie Carvalko, Senior Acquisitions Editor, Psychology, Health, and Social Work, for her helpful suggestions and her availability for assistance when needed.

1 ▪ ▪ ▪

The Multifaceted Nature of Control

If I am in control,
I can do and get what I want
I will not be embarrassed, ridiculed, or shamed
I will win the arguments and competition
I can predict my days
My decisions and actions will not be questioned
. . .
I will not be denied!

Those are statements expressing individuals' expectations about being in control, but confronting the promises' excitement, others fearfully point to the restrictions and constraints when control is in the hands of their adversaries.

Control attempts are everywhere, and sooner or later everybody will be affected by control schemes—the web of manipulation is of global proportions and stretches into the farthest corners. The players in this gigantic web are the manipulators, the targets, and the victims. Some targets become victims, and others may be spared victimization through coincidence (some might want to call it fate) or because their own actions prevent or curtail victimization. Then there are the super-victims, those who through their own compulsive need for control become the targets of self-victimization.

Whether control strivings are motivated by ambition, desire for freedom from responsibility, or fear, they are competitive in nature. Ambition leads to wanting more than the next person has, the wish for freedom from responsibility is rooted in wanting to do less than others, and fear is based on wanting to be as safe, or safer, than those who have more power and can crush them physically or emotionally. How is control over others established, executed, and maintained? In those win-lose situations of competition it is only a matter of time until simple persuasion turns to deception with its lies and betrayals, creeping in and corrupting the competitive strivings.

What amounts to control and/or manipulation often is in the eyes of the beholder. What some people experience as a measure of control placed upon them, others may regard as part of a normal orderly process or routine that has been accepted and taken for granted over time. What makes some people reject strongly even the slightest control processes and what causes others to quietly accept or even welcome the presence of control measures? We find the answer to this question in the large variety of control approaches and the wide range of people's responses to them.

Control has many faces and comes in many disguises. In the introduction to her book, *Imperfect Control: Our Lifelong Struggle with Power and Surrender,* Judith Viorst (1998) described control as the capacity to manage, master, dominate, exercise power over, regulate, influence, curb, suppress, or restrain. Thus, control can be as simple as the desire to follow one's own will, making decisions instead of having others decide, or—by wanting to master one's environment—it may include the mastery of other people within that environment. Control issues are central factors in our political and economic lives. In our personal and professional relationships as well, we see ourselves defined by the levels and positions of control inherent in everyday situations: some we accept; others we chafe against.

The type of control that comes most readily to mind is that of manipulation, which carries a range of meanings from treatment and handling to exploitation. Most generally, however, it is used in the sense of manipulation as the control exerted over other persons to one's own advantage. It is also the type of control people become aware of most readily. While we are focusing on the more malevolent aspects of controlling behaviors, we often miss less obvious attempts at control. Perhaps in more common and obvious ways, control dynamics can be observed to operate along the cultural lines of authority and subtle coercion found in the status differentials between employee and supervisor and between men and women. In the larger context many aspects of our lives are governed or controlled by social and cultural rules. Control systems that appear to be sanctioned by society are usually accepted by individuals and—with time—come to be expected in certain settings.

▓ Controlling the Environment as Means of Controlling Others

Arrangements of environmental or situational factors can function as less obvious methods of control because they often veil the instigator. Take for instance, museums or palaces with roped off areas. The public is not allowed to come closer to an art object or a piece of antique furniture than is indicated by the ropes. Most individuals obey those nonverbal directions, assuming that some government official or museum curator/director has decided on this space for the protection and conservation of irreplaceable treasures. We are socialized to obey the rules of such environmental directives without questioning.

This type of socializing provides effective training for other situations, too. When entering a physician's or an attorney's office, for instance, the high-backed chair at the other side of the big desk communicates "off limits" to the visitor. Instead, there are two or three side chairs placed on the side of the desk opposite the "big" chair. The big chair is placed with its back in front of a window so that visitors face the light, often squinting, while the face of the office occupant remains in the shadow. Of course, the desk itself functions as a barrier to keep visitors in their place. Parallel to the function of the window just described, light fixtures can be arranged to yield similar effects of control.

Nothing works better for establishing and maintaining social and cultural rules than rituals. The practice of rituals serves to obscure or eliminate any doubts about the "correctness" of the control dynamics. In fact, the duration of its very existence over generations is usually taken as evidence for the properness of a given control system. Rituals incorporate and legitimize rules of conduct for various situations. Individuals are obligated to behave in certain ways and conversely, certain behaviors are expected of them by others. People of lower social standing are expected to behave in deferential ways toward those of higher social standing. The person neglecting to fulfill those expectations usually pays a price.

▓ Expectations and Their Controlling Effects

Expectations that significant others have of us can also function as control-exerting aspects on our behavior, although the specific strength of the influence may vary depending on the way these expectations are expressed. Furthermore, relating to the degree of the person's significance in our lives, our behaviors will follow the person's expectations of us. The more important the person is to us the less we would want to disappoint those expectations.

On the other hand, expectations can also have a controlling effect on those who hold certain expectations of others. Psychologist Robert Rosenthal (2002) investigated how—what he called—interpersonal expectancy effects operate in the facilitation of self-fulfilling prophecies. Rosenthal reported on a laboratory study with psychology students in which participants were shown a series of 10 photographs of people's faces with the instruction to rate each individual in the photographs according to their likely level of success or failure. Embedded in the instructions were bits of "information" conveying whether the persons in the photographs were socially well established or were unsuccessful. Not surprisingly, the participants' ratings reflected a significant level of agreement with the information that they had detected in the instructions.

Similar findings were obtained in studies involving animal experiments. Student experimenters, who believed that the animals they were working with were bright, reported daily improvements in the animals' performance. Those animals believed to be dull seemed to improve initially, only to demonstrate deteriorating performances afterward. At the end of the experiment, participants were requested to rate their rats' performance and their own attitudes toward their animals. Those student experimenters who had been led to expect better performance described their animals as being brighter and more likeable than the animals they had expected to perform poorly. Their own attitudes toward the animals confirmed the expectations they held about them. Contact with those animals expected to perform well was relaxed and friendly according to the participants' statements.

These findings were taken a step further in the design of the Pygmalion experiment, involving students and teachers in a South San Francisco school district. Although the details of the design are too elaborate to describe here, the results are relevant to the content of this book. In summary, at the end of the school year, designated as the study period for the experiment, teachers were asked for descriptions of their pupils' classroom behavior. Those children who were expected to show intellectual growth were described as interesting, curious, well-adjusted, and promising a successful future.

The study included a control group of children who were not given special expectations. Although some of these undesignated children in the control group showed intellectual gains, their teachers did not rate them any more favorably. The pupils who were expected to perform well may have benefited from their teachers' expectations, but those children who achieved progress in the absence of encouraging expectations did so perhaps out of their own motivational system. Their intellectual growth apparently went unnoticed by their teachers. This observation confirms the saying: "You don't get a second chance to make a first impression," and it does not seem to make a difference whether we are dealing with children or rats.

On the basis of his investigations, Rosenthal proposed a four-factor theory of the mediation of teacher expectancy effects. The four factors refer to categories of teacher behaviors. For instance, the first factor, climate, describes the socioemotional climate that teachers tend to create for their pupils, depending on their expectations for them. The teachers' tendency to teach more material to students of whom they have high expectations, Rosenthal called the input factor. In addition, teachers apparently also have a tendency to provide more opportunities for responding to questions to their high-expectancy pupils, which is defined as the output factor. The fourth factor, called the feedback factor, refers to the teachers' tendency to give more differentiated feedback—usually based directly on the student's particular response—to their high-expectancy students.

In analyzing studies applying the four-factor theory, Rosenthal found the effects for the climate and input factors were especially impressive. The investigator's conclusion was that teachers seemed to be more invested in teaching more and in a warmer manner to students of whom they had favorable expectations. In other words, the teachers' behaviors were controlled by their own expectations of the various students in their care. It does not take a giant leap to imagine the application of Rosenthal's findings to the fields of advertising and marketing, as will be seen in a later chapter.

The experiments described above demonstrate how people's expectations of others—humans or animals—influence their thoughts and behavior toward them. To a degree, our own expectations control how we view those around us. Gatherings at large family holidays present a stage for the observation of interesting interplays of expectations and disappointments. When the number of invited guests extends past the hostesses' capacity to provide all the ingredients for the feast, guests' contributions, such as a salad, a side dish, or a desert, are a common solution to the challenge. Hosts may expect a satisfactory variety of food items to arrive with the guests; they may also expect that the guests will take only their empty dishes with them when they leave the celebration.

With that expectation, the hosts will leave all the food on the table without supervising everybody's intake. Some guests may expect returning to their home with the remaining parts of the food items they originally contributed, whereas other guests' expectations include leaving with generous packages of leftover food items, sampled from all the available delicacies—even though they themselves may have contributed very little or nothing to the feast. Because the food had been donated by several individuals or families, those who expect to help themselves to the leftovers may not feel a need to ask permission from the host or every contributing individual (Martin, 2009a). Obviously, if all involved act on their expectations, their goals constitute a mutual conflict, and their individual behaviors will create discomfort that might well destroy the expected harmonious atmosphere of the event. Who is going to control the dynamics of the various expectations and their outcomes in reality?

Being blinded by one's expectations can have costlier outcomes than what happens to the leftovers of a family feast. Joanne, a 24-year-old, green-eyed brunette, had found the man of her dreams, she announced to her friends. Anthony bore a physical resemblance to the movie star George Clooney, and Joanne thought she detected similar qualities in Anthony that she had admired in Clooney's characterization in some of the movies she saw. Without being aware of it, Joanne expected Anthony to be similar in character and behavior to what she saw portrayed in Clooney's roles. While she focused on the expected facets in Anthony's behavior, other behavioral aspects seemed less relevant, and she did not make a mental note of them. Her expectations also shaped her own behaviors. Because he seemed so wonderful, she was happy, charming, and loving; she did everything she could to please him.

After almost five months of dating, Anthony mentioned future plans that included a commitment in the form of an engagement. When he presented Joanne with the model of the engagement ring that he had considered giving her, she was speechless. The model was forged of sterling silver, which was supposed to be platinum in the end product. A center diamond, almost three carats in size—cubic zirconia in the model—was flanked by two smaller bluish-white diamonds, all held together within an intricate scroll-like setting that tapered into a plain platinum band. It was a breathtaking sight. Joanne tried on the model; it fit perfectly. Did she like the ring, Anthony asked, explaining that the reason for the model was his wish to make sure that the ring would please her.

Joanne's expectations of receiving this gorgeous piece of jewelry may have prompted her to agree to an early official engagement to be followed by a wedding—all within less than a year. While the jeweler worked on the "real" engagement ring, Joanne was allowed to wear the model. Although the jeweler had a copy of the model, several difficulties developed that slowed down the production. The copy of the model had been misplaced. Then the primary artisan to work on this masterpiece suffered from some mysterious illness. These were only the beginning difficulties; other problems popped up and delayed the appearance of the final product.

At her engagement party Joanne still wore the model, but it would only be a matter of days for the final version to be ready, she explained to her guests. Anthony suggested they work on establishing their future home, so that it would be ready for them to move in after their honeymoon. He reasoned that they could select the basic equipment and furniture they would need and have it placed in the new home before they left for their honeymoon. Then, as he explained to Joanne, they could relax while on their

honeymoon. Upon their return, Anthony would follow the traditional cus-
tom of carrying Joanne over the first threshold of their married life.

It sounded so romantic, and Joanne's attention was devoted to the
many aspects of their wedding, honeymoon, and the preparations for their
future home. Anthony explained that in order to have everything develop
as planned they needed to pool their financial resources and get started
immediately. Anthony's plans sounded so sincere and convincing that
Joanne's parents handed over a sizeable amount of cash to add to Joanne's
own savings.

The difficulties with the engagement ring were only the beginning;
other problems with their overall grandiose planning occurred. Some of
them—the smaller ones—got resolved rather easily; others seemed to linger
on. Anthony pointed out how smart they had been to start early with
these preparations. Every day would make a difference in the probability
of getting the important details taken care of. Then there came a time
when Joanne's family received a significant number of communications
from the sources involved in the wedding-honeymoon-new home scenario.
Many of them mentioned that the money to be paid in advance was over-
due. Unless payments were received at a certain date, the preparations
would be stopped.

Anthony was not available for answers. He had been out of town on business for the past week. In his most recent e-mail to Joanne he had mentioned that he might have to stay another week to be able to wind up the
business activities he was engaged in. Phone calls to the hotel he was staying in were more disturbing—Anthony had checked out two days before,
with no forwarding address. His landlady in town informed Joanne that
Anthony's lease had expired and he had not renewed it because he was getting married. There were very few personal belongings in Anthony's apartment. Information from Anthony's employer revealed that Anthony had
resigned his job, explaining that he was getting married and expected to
work for his future father-in-law in Alabama—or was it Georgia? The manager was not sure. Anthony was well liked, and his resignation came as a
sad surprise, the manager added. In fact, some of his coworkers had given
Anthony a bachelor party before he left.

To summarize the end of Joanne's sad experience: she was left with the
model for the engagement ring minus the financial resources she and her
parents had contributed to the situation. There were no legal papers
signed that could be used in enforcing restitution of their losses. Without
a doubt, Anthony had taken advantage of Joanne and her parents, and the
engagement ring model served as a control tactic in his overall scheme.
Engagement rings work well in manipulating women's attention and perception because they represent a symbol of commitment, and as such they
entice women to believe in the symbol rather than investigate reality. As
there is no legal contract attached to the symbol, its real significance lies

in the fantasy, the fantasy of Mr. Wonderful having made a commitment to matrimony.

Joanne's own expectations of Anthony had led her to look for what she wanted to find in him rather than what was really there. Were there any indications of possible dishonesty? Joanne admitted that there had been some contradictions or incongruent parts in the overall picture Anthony presented. However, Joanne had explained them away as forgetfulness or too many things going on during the hectic days of their courtship. Her expectations of Anthony found their beginning in his resemblance to a movie star and were confirmed with his presentation of the engagement ring model. Those two factors represented the foundation for her expectations of a romantic relationship, ending in marriage to a wonderful man. Once her expectations were formed, she did not require any deeper examination of the man and his background.

▮ The Deception-Expectation Alliance

Considering control issues, most people think of schemes with which some people control others to their own advantage or a picture of a person obsessed with control around him or her—what is commonly called a control "freak" may come to mind. While deception can play a role in the first scenario, it is not a prominent feature of the second situation, the control freak's life. In the market place, however, people are used to encountering control attempts through advertising that may contain various degrees of deception about a particular product or service. Deception, as an act of "controlling information to alter the target's beliefs or understanding in a way that the deceiver knows is false" (Buller & Burgoon, 1994, p. 192), is a basic element of many control schemes. By providing untrue information to the target person, the victim's decisions are directed by the instigator of the deception.

A blatant example of how deception controls the lifestyles of others can be found in Bernard Madoff's Ponzi scheme that not long ago received wide attention in the public eye. His operating mode was in part based on people's greed and on people's desire to be special in some ways. Because he made it appear that investing with him was a privilege, reserved for a chosen few, they were eager to hand over millions of dollars to him. The privilege came at a high price. Along with numerous other investors, even his closest friends came to feel Madoff's control over their lifestyles when they lost everything they had in the big scheme. The victims' sobs, screams, and curses could be heard in Aspen, Palm Beach, and New York; a "roar echoed through homes, offices, and institutions worldwide. But it was too late; by then Bernie Madoff and $50 billion were gone" (Seal, 2009, p. 173).

As Joanne's story and the research reports above indicate, expectations, our own as well as those of others, can control our perceptions and shape our thoughts and actions. By the same token, as the studies demonstrate, expectations can be manipulated through acts of deception and misinformation. Deception aimed at arousing certain expectations in target individuals presents a particularly dangerous linkage because in a way it persuades the targets to actively participate in their own victimization. Because of his deceptive tactics, Madoff's victims expected that by investing their financial resources with him they would become richer faster than anybody else investing with others. Their expectations prompted them to willingly part with their money.

As emphasized by David Livingstone Smith, professor of philosophy, human beings can think of many ways to deceive. "We *Homo sapiens* are able to lie across the board. Furthermore, we use these gifts to manipulate our own kind, enemies and friends, lovers and rivals, parents and children" (2004, p. 49). It is apparent then that control in its many forms is an ever-present factor in our lives. Being aware of its existence in its many facets and understanding the dynamics of it are just the initial steps in our experiences with control. How to use control wisely and how to protect oneself from the damaging effects of others' harmful control attempts require additional efforts and learning.

▦ Deception in the Marketplace

Researchers in the area of deception in the marketplace have come up with examples describing various deception strategies that modern consumers face every day (Boush, Friestad, & Wright, 2009). Out of the list of 16 examples, at least half of them can be and have been applied in noncommerce interpersonal relationships. To assist consumers in their self-protective actions, the researchers have highlighted several theoretical foundations underlying deceptive behaviors that promote the understanding and awareness of such schemes and lead to improved deception detection and protection skills in the consumers.

Research involving everyday lie telling has focused on cues lay people use in detecting deception. Most of these lies are constructed on the spot without preparation or rehearsing. Only occasionally are these types of lies told for material gains; mostly they exist for momentary personal convenience or increased importance of self. Investment in detecting cues about these lies is usually not as important to most people, but in contrast to the everyday lie-telling individual, experienced marketers use top-down planning of the complete deception campaigns. They select their plans from a range of different tactics and different ways of executing methods. They pretest, revise, practice, and refine their strategies. They go so far as to have contingency plans ready to draw upon. It is not unusual for individuals engaged in interpersonal control schemes to invest the same amount of effort into their strategies as do the marketing control experts. Thus, it would seem reasonable for those who want to avoid being taken advantage of to invest just as much effort and energy in observing the signs, the pattern, the techniques, and the goals of the deception agents.

A significant element in deception as well as other control scenarios is the power of persuasion. Different types of persuasion strategies exist that are particularly suited to dealing with different targets and achieving various goals. In a later chapter discussing control schemes in advertising and business, the various persuasion techniques will be examined in greater detail.

▓ Theoretical Views of Control Behaviors

Controlling behaviors—like all other behaviors—can be understood through the theoretical inclination of the observer. An interesting analogy drawn by Richard Marken (2002), a behavioral scientist at the Rand Corporation, suggested that different theoretical inclinations function in a way like prescription glasses worn by the observer. In particular, the author distinguished between two different approaches of perception. One approach involved scientific psychologists adhering to a causal explanation of perceived behavior such as internal or external stimuli causing the behavior and another approach, favoring the notion that behavior is purposeful (Gelman, Durgin, & Kaufman, 1995; Premack, 1990).

For instance, a person entering a bathroom may do so because of the urgings of his or her bladder. This event can be understood as caused by an internal stimulus, such as the person's bladder communicating that it is stretched to capacity. Another person may approach a bathroom following a companion's statement about a smudge of dirt on the person's face. Here the observed bathroom approach would appear to be caused by an external stimulus: the other person's remark.

On the other hand, the notion that behavior is purposeful is reflected in what Marken (1992) called the control theory prescription approach, because the observer seems to interpret a person's efforts to produce outcomes or results as purposeful. While causal theory assumes that behavioral output is caused by an external or internal stimulus event, in control theory the internal purposes are considered to be specifications for perceptual input. Seen through control theory glasses, intentional behavior is described, not as caused output, but as controlled input, the input being the control of perception on the part of the behaving organism. In the bathroom example, the person would be thought to have perceived the message of his or her bladder and decided it was time for a bathroom visit or the person had perceived the verbal statement about the dirt on his or her face and decided to head for the bathroom to wash it off.

Assuming that the behavior under observation represents the person's effort to control some aspect of his or her own perceptual experience, one can test this hypothesis through control theory glasses. By focusing on the so-called controlled variable, a specified behavior demonstrated by the person under observation, one can disturb the flow of the behavior, or the function of the controlled variable, and note whether or not there are any changes in the controlled variable.

Building on Marken's use of the concept of "personal space" as a controlled variable, one could conceive of a situation where a person (A) might take a few steps closer to another person (B), who would feel uncomfortable about the diminishing personal space. If B acts on the feeling of discomfort and takes a few steps back to reinstate the original size of the space and A remains at the current position, person B would interpret that to mean that A had not been aware of B's preference but also had no intentions of making B feel uncomfortable.

If, on the other hand, person A again takes a few steps closer to person B and remains in that position for as long as B remains there, on the basis of these observations B might conclude that A had intended to invade B's personal space as a matter of control or of demonstrating A's power. Person B can continue the observation by moving away again; if A continues to approach, B would confirm the suspicions about A's intention to manipulate the situation and to discomfort B by invading B's personal space.

Control Techniques

Techniques used in controlling behaviors are numerous and vary in their application: aggressive behavior, displays of emotions such as anger, resentment and threats, suicide attempts, tears, withdrawal, silence, sensitivity, passivity, sarcasm, criticism, promises, smiles, questioning, interrogating, bragging, lying, soliciting, begging, and many others. The list is endless. Some items on this list are normally not considered to be of a controlling nature. However, in reality, all of human behavior is controlling in some way although we don't pay much attention to the controlling behaviors of others unless it appears that we have been taken advantage of in some unfair scheme. In fact, often our feelings may signal to us before our brains tell us that something is not quite right.

There is overlap in the use of control techniques, because individuals do not necessarily employ just one technique exclusively. Therefore, if we are in a position to observe the various techniques used by a person, we can usually outline a particular pattern of techniques that matches with a particular constellation of personality traits.

As pervasive and limitless as situations of control are in our lives, so are the techniques employed in the execution of control, and—most likely—there are just as many control techniques that miscarry as there are methods that can be worked successfully. Throughout the book there will be opportunities to study both. For those who think they need it, it would be wise to recognize that it is better to learn handling control than seizing it or getting it by default.

The wide range of control techniques justifies devoting a whole chapter to their discussion. Examples of their use will help readers to become aware of many of those techniques. The ability to recognize the techniques used, provides opportunities for avoiding or reducing their intended impact.

Control on a Larger Scale: Groups

Our lives are not spent in a vacuum and the influence of others in our environment cannot be overestimated. This influence becomes even more powerful for those who have chosen or have been chosen to become members of particular groups. Whether the groups are professional groups or are bound together by common interests, their influence on the individual can be significant.

When considering group influences within a reality-based framework, questions about the types of behavior that will facilitate an individual's inclusion in meaningful groups and about the way individuals make their behavioral decisions come to mind. Studies with college students have suggested that students making behavioral decisions based on concerns of social desirability will assign greater values to the perceived social consequences of these behaviors if the behaviors positively distinguish the individual's self-concept from similar others in their social group (Blanton & Christie, 2003). On the surface this would seem contrary to expectations gained from considering the literature on reference groups, which suggests that reference groups encourage conformity.

In general, reference groups make it clear what is expected of their members. Those potential members who comply with the expectations are thought to value the group and may be eligible for inclusion into the group. However, this conformity with the group's expectations and norms does not reflect an individual's desire to seek a positive self-concept as much as a desire to avoid a negative identity, and thus it functions as a negative reward structure. The negative incentive system operates in many groups that seek uniformity of action. The pressure to conform to the group's norms is usually expressed as social punishment against those who deviate from the norms; it is not articulated as a reward to those who conform.

College fraternities and sororities encourage uniformity of action among students. The desire to be chosen for the in-group influences students to make gifts to or perform services for the popular members of the sorority or fraternity in order to be accepted. However, reference groups not only have norms regarding what members should do to be accepted, but there also are actions that are desired by the group but that are not necessarily required of each member. These are idealized behaviors, not required behaviors, and they provide opportunities for individuals to positively distinguish themselves from others in the group. Most fraternities and sororities require uniformity of action but also have space to accommodate idealized behaviors.

Within this theoretical framework, a dual-motivational system that structures the pursuit of a meaningful identity within an accepted reference group could be conceived of where equal emphasis is given to both motivations (Blanton & Christie, 2003). The pursuit of a positive identity is favored in some social contexts, while in other contexts the avoidance of a negative identity is favored. Which one of the two incentive systems is going to determine actions would be dependent on individual and contextual factors. Taking the needs of both self-regulatory systems into account, the highest levels of self-esteem would be achieved by those who avoid all the negatives required by their reference groups and who are also successful in achieving some of the optional ideals desired by their reference groups. "By living up to the oughts, people avoid exclusion. By achieving some of the ideals, people gain praise and admiration" (Blanton & Christie, 2003, p. 130).

Thus, groups provide opportunities as well as controlling guidelines for individuals to develop and modify their view of themselves within the framework of what a particular group requires and what it desires. However, the degree of control or power that groups exert on their individual members is also a function of the beliefs shared by the group members. The more members identify with the beliefs and values of their group, the more likely it is that the individual members accept the beliefs as basic truths not subject to challenges or doubts. The level of conviction individual group members hold for their group's beliefs determines in part the degree of power the group has over its members because the members' strength of conviction in essence bestows the controlling power on the group.

Exploration of various belief domains held both by individuals and groups could provide information about the way the intersections of joint belief domains might affect the individual's identification with the group and the willingness to act on the group's behalf (Eidelson & Eidelson, 2003). The researchers selected the factor superiority as the first of the core beliefs. People who believe in their own superiority hold on to attitudes of specialness and entitlements. Thus, in a narcissistic way, these individuals may disregard societal rules because their own perceived specialness places them above others. Usually their efforts are focused on their own aggrandizement, without wasting energies on considering the opinions of those around them.

On the group level, attitudes of superiority lead to the formation of exclusivity in groups, such as can be observed in class-based groups, ethnically based identity groups, or certain religion-based groups, fundamentalist groups, or cults. An exaggerated sense of group entitlement bestows on its members a sense of having been chosen, which is often interpreted as the right to rule or control others outside the group. The chosen ones feel invested with a moral responsibility to uphold and defend the laws and judgments of the particular group.

At almost the opposite end of the spectrum are those who see themselves as having been treated unfairly in life. Individuals who carry with them the core belief of injustice perceive themselves as victims of persecution and mistreatment by specific others. Carrying this attitude to the extreme, individuals conceive of injustice and victimization wherever they go. They feel that others will intentionally harm them or take advantage of them if given a chance, and this is a constant concern. Therefore, it is essential to keep control over situations so that there will be no chance for others to carry out their supposedly harmful actions toward the distrusting individual. The core belief of distrust ranges from having a predisposition toward suspicion to outright paranoia with delusions of persecution. As the level of distrust increases, so will the vigilant obsession with control. The feeling of constantly being threatened with no guarantee for security can lead to disastrous actions, such as gang wars on a community level or revolutions on a global level.

On a group level, the collective mindset of distrust functions as a central element in universal stereotyping of out-groups. Compared with individuals constituting the in-group, those who belong to different groups cannot be trusted for various reasons. There is usually a list of handy explanations for the lack of trustworthiness of the out-groups. For instance, Protestants might say "you can't trust Catholics to be honest because they go to confession regularly and are absolved of all their sins. They don't need to be honest." In medieval Europe, it was widely believed that Jews were dishonest and greedy because they were moneylenders, but the stereotypes did not take into consideration that the religious laws of that time forced the Jews to be moneylenders because Christians were not allowed to engage in such activities and Jews' occupations were limited to certain kinds of work.

Whether on the individual level or on the group level, core beliefs can function to empower individuals to search for ways to control what is perceived as being uncontrollable either by preparation for defense or by direct retaliation. Strongly held core beliefs are deeply entrenched in peoples' minds and become part of their character or personality constellations. Becoming a member of a particular group can thus be regarded as an expression of a particular individual's personality.

In general, as individuals, people hold the same values and beliefs as they do as members of a larger group. Individual-level core beliefs and collective worldviews of the groups they are members of seem to operate in tandem (Eidelson & Eidelson, 2003). Individual beliefs can be inferred from the beliefs and attitudes of the groups the individual belongs to. Similarly, people's behaviors and coping mechanisms function in parallel ways in both individual actions and in collective actions. The exception may be the manner and degree of the group's influence on facilitating or inhibiting certain activities through the dynamics of diffused responsibility and assumption of a mass identity rather than individual identity of its members.

Individuals, who feel they are special and therefore are entitled to an elevated position and treatment in life, seldom receive as much as they think they deserve. As a result, they will believe that they are not receiving fair treatment. Consequently, they will consider it their obligation to see to it that they get what is rightly theirs. In order to retain their special status, they have to control as best they can that others remain at lower levels socially, intellectually, morally, or whatever variables are functioning in providing the exclusive position to those chosen ones.

Avoiding loss of control is the focus for individuals with attitudes of superiority, injustice, vulnerability, and distrust. For the person holding a superiority belief achieving or maintaining the entitlement that is connected to a high position becomes the center of control; defending one's rights becomes the obsession of the person with an attitude of injustice. Those concerned with their own vulnerability spend their efforts guarding their own security, and similarly, the distrustful people vigilantly watch out to keep others from taking advantage of them.

▨ Control within the Self

Those who strive to be the masters of their own fate, who act independently and responsibly in maintaining their sense of self-fulfillment and self-determination, exercise a different type of control. Theirs is a system of control that can contain dignity for themselves and for those around them. Because of the all-pervasiveness of control, it stands to reason that a comprehensive coverage of the topic will include aspects of self-control as well as aspects of control exerted by others. The lesson starts with looking inward and begins with achieving self-control. Those who strive to be the masters of their own fate, who act independently and responsibly in maintaining their sense of self-determination, apply a system of control that can contain dignity for themselves and for those around them.

Mastering self-control includes as many opportunities for failure as does mastering control over others. In order to achieve this system of control with dignity, it is necessary to become familiar with the others, so as to recognize the various techniques and to reduce or avoid one's participation in any strategies that inflict harm on self or others. Control within self is based on the assumption that individuals can be in charge of their own thoughts, feelings, words, and actions. With what is commonly known as "self-discipline," individuals can learn to master their behaviors and to take control of their lives. Controlling one's life means being aware of the temptation of excuses and procrastination and to resist the temptation to indulge in them. Controlling one's life also includes the establishment of goals that are realistic and well defined. Goals provide direction and meaning for actions. Self-discipline includes the mastery of goal management through monitoring and reviewing the progress toward the desired outcomes:

> The art of mastering self-discipline is not a journey of sacrifice or deprivation, but one of control and focus. The power to manage, understand, and focus your physical and mental talents towards a determined goal or lifestyle is not meant to restrict or deprive an individual of pleasure and fun, but rather to enhance these enjoyable experiences. The object of mastering self-discipline is to increase the amount of pleasure and decrease the amount of pain you experience, through the process of controlling your thoughts, actions, emotions, and future. (Janke, 2000, p.107)

Similar to the ways that rituals maintain systems of control within the community, individuals create routines to achieve a sense of security and control in their daily lives. "Routines become a protective mechanism against the uncertainty and constant change of everyday life. In order to minimize the effects of change and uncertainty in our lives, we build routines to give us a sense of control" (p. 165).

Contemplation of control within the individual includes a wide range of aspects and can be understood as a work in progress as the individual discovers, learns, applies, and modifies the many variables that compose the framework of the person's sense of being in control. The final chapter of this book is devoted to explorations of this significant topic.

Any considerations about control sooner or later come up against moral judgments, such as what type of control and how much of it is good or bad? Are the motives of the person exerting control good or bad? What control strategies are benevolent in nature and which ones are expressions of evilness? There are no well-defined answers to these questions that will apply to all situations. In fact, individuals will have to judge and decide for themselves what is good and what is bad according to their own value system.

2 ▦ ▦ ▦

Origins and Development of Control Attempts

Infancy provides the stage for most individuals to launch their first attempts at controlling the environment. Gaining control is the infant's first task soon after arrival in this world. As their ability to respond to the environment develops, infants learn how to elicit desirable behaviors from those around them. The infants' targets are the parents or other caregivers, and their goals are to get what they want; the consequences are yet to be experienced and learned from.

▦ Early Practice of Controlling Behaviors

As control attempts start in infancy, learning begins with the first time the baby accidentally drops a toy, which then miraculously reappears within the baby's reach due to the help of the adult caregiver. This learning experience calls for further exploration. When the toy falls to the ground again, the event is less accidental and becomes more calculated. Will the toy appear again within the infant's reach? If it does, the baby may have learned that objects falling to the ground can rise miraculously.

This hypothesis can be tested easily by dropping the object again. If the toy or object does not reappear within the infant's reach, the baby's next move is to cry. When the adult provides the toy again, the infant learns that the act of crying has become an instrument of control. At the same time, the smart little baby is learning the difference between magic and actions such as crying, which he or she can perform to exert control. For a while crying provides a powerful mechanism in summoning the presence of adults for many purposes, such as feeding, cleaning, comforting, playing, and entertaining.

Some consider control to be a main source of happiness, which begins early in life (Parrott, 2000). In an experiment, 8-week-old babies were placed on special air pillows that responded to the pressure from the babies' heads by closing a switch. The infants were divided into three groups. For the infants in one group a mobile with colored balls started spinning over the infant's crib as soon as the pillow was pressed. The mobile's movement lasted for about one second. The babies of the second group also saw a spinning mobile over their cribs, but the spinning of the mobiles was unrelated to the infants' actions. For the third group the mobile was replaced by a stable arrangement so that the infants of this group experienced neither movement nor control. The results showed that the infants of the first group significantly increased the number of times they pressed the pillow after they had learned that they could control the movements of the mobile. The infants of the other two groups did not show an increase in pillow-pressing activity. Furthermore, the infants in the first group were smiling and cooing three or four days after the start of the experiment (Seligman, 1975).

Prolonged successful control of the environment requires the ability to adapt. As the child grows older, crying might prove to be a less efficient tool of control than it was earlier, but some children will still increase their crying efforts in intensity, duration, and frequency. When success in bringing about the desired condition does not materialize, children may develop fears and insecurities or they may find different means to interact with their environment. Those children, who search for other ways to obtain helpful responses from their environment, develop a crucial insight: they can make things happen.

▓ Laying the Foundations for Personality Patterns

Developmental researchers have suggested that children who tend to do things for themselves may feel a sense of triumph as a result of their interactions with the environment (Masten & Coatsworth, 1998). They also experience a sense of mastery as they continue their successful interactions with the world around them. Mastery, as a gratifying exchange with one's environment, leads to increased motivation for interacting and to optimistic expectations of future control. Competence, the belief in being able to master or control, develops as the child adjusts to the changing environment and achieves developmental tasks.

For some, however, the developmental tasks of adjusting to changing environments are difficult to master, and they may instead devote all their energies to maintaining absolute control of all aspects of their environment instead of learning to adapt to changes. They become so obsessed with being in control that changes will affect them in disturbing ways, leading to high anxiety and anger, expressed as crying and temper tantrums in childhood and as threats, demands, angry outbursts, or withdrawal in adulthood.

Thus, the foundations of personality patterns are laid early on in childhood, although this does not mean that they are inflexible and not subject to modification. Basically we can distinguish between those children who learn to make things happen and those who learn to make other people do for them. Infants who get their needs met through crying and graduating to temper tantrums can be recognized as adults who passively expect wishes to be fulfilled and who resort to complaining when their expectations are disappointed. The method of control exerted upon the environment here is complaint, which parallels the crying used in infancy and the temper tantrums of later childhood and adolescence. Those individuals who in childhood felt rewarded in their attempts to obtain desired objects through their own activity (other than crying) will likely adopt methods of control that are independent and self-sufficient in nature.

Methods of control developed in childhood do not only operate in situations of gaining and obtaining things, but also find application in situations of avoidance. In fact, some researchers consider individuals' avoidance strategies as being of equal importance to gaining and obtaining in the person's personality pattern. More than a quarter of a century ago, as a way of expanding understanding of a person's lifestyle, Kefir (1981) proposed the concept of personality priorities that function as avoidance strategies. Individuals have their own methods of moving away from a perceived traumatic event in order to gain a sense of control over fear and chaos. According to this view, the key to understanding an individual's personality pattern lies in knowing what the person wishes to avoid.

Most of us know people who are uncomfortable when facing confrontations of any kind. Janet hated to face waitresses in restaurants when it came time to pay the bill. In her young adult years as a poor student she worked as a waitress to help with her tuition. Thinking back on those years, Janet was tempted to leave an especially generous tip for young waitresses who reminded her of her past struggle. Tom, her husband, had a way of criticizing Janet's generosity in a sarcastic manner. Yet, if she left a smaller tip, she felt the waitress looking at her accusingly. To avoid both her husband's criticism and her own guilt feelings, Janet seldom went to restaurants by herself but arranged to be with friends. Upon her urging they would split the bill in half and with that the other person would usually determine the amount of the tip. In order to make sure that her companions would be willing to share the costs of the meal, Janet had to select items from the menu that were the same as or slightly below the price for the other person's meal.

Unlike other control attempts, Janet's avoidance-related control maneuvers did not place other people at a disadvantage. Her lack of confidence in her own decision-making skills prompted her to avoid confrontations with her husband, and to ease her own discomfort confronting the waitress, she persuaded others to make the decision for her without hurting those others. In the long run those avoidance techniques might put Janet at a disadvantage because she deprives herself of visiting a restaurant by herself, and because of the necessary vigilance to make sure that her meals are at the same price as those of her companions, she limits her meal selection.

■ Parents' Control Strategies

Parents apply their own methods of control over aspects of their children's lives. Some methods are successful; others result in the children's rebellion. Under the pretext of wanting what is in their children's best interest, parents exert their influences on such important issues as their children's career choices and marriages, as well as such smaller issues as what friends to have, what to wear, and what extracurricular activities to engage in. How many children practice playing the piano for hours on end without wanting to, compared with those who do the same but of their own volition? We don't know the answer; national surveys have neglected this topic as of yet.

Parents, who attempt to live vicariously through their children's lives, exert control over their children's entire lifestyle. The cliché about the stage mother comes readily to mind. An image we are all familiar with is that of women who did not have the opportunity to become dancers, actresses, singers, or beauty queens, dragging their little daughters into the offices of agents, talent scouts, and producers. If we don't see it in our neighborhood, we read about it in the magazines that thrive on the personal accounts of the lives of popular female performers.

Fathers, who try to recapture their own ambitions vicariously through their sons' lives, do not receive such a widespread attention, yet they are just as prevalent. There are many fathers who want their sons to follow in their footsteps, by taking over their businesses, their medical or law practices, and to become at least as successful as the fathers were. And then there are those fathers who for whatever reasons were not able to fulfill their own aspirations but see a second chance in the lives of their sons. The male adventurer, who wanted to explore distant shores and unknown parts of the world but who became an accountant instead and raised a family, may be the one who takes his young son fishing and hunting and teaches him the art and skills of self-defense. He may take him camping and teach the son how to pitch a tent, how to build a fire, and how to clean and cook the fish they just caught.

He may be the father who takes his son out on the boat most weekends and teaches him how to navigate by the light of the stars in the night sky. He teaches him to pay attention to the wind and be aware of the changes in strength and direction and how to respond to them. While father and son are sitting by the fire or in the cozy space of their boat's cabin, the father talks about the excitement of exploring uncharted territory and encountering unknown dangers, but overcoming them successfully. Those are wonderful experiences that fathers and sons can share. They are great opportunities to forge close emotional bonds between fathers and sons, and they are valuable teachable moments when fathers can pass on signifi-cant life skills to their sons.

Nobody could find fault with such a close bonding between father and son—except for the one-sidedness of their joint activities. Does the same father just as caringly help in the development of the son's academic inter-ests? Does he just as gently nurture the son's philosophical inquiries? Does he expose him to literary works, concerts, ballets, museums, and theatrical productions? And, even more significantly, does he include female siblings in their activities? Does the father guide his son in getting along in the heterosexual world that he lives in or is he constructing the image of a world that is a solitary and introverted male world, perhaps a dream world the father would have wanted for himself but did not have the opportunity or courage to create for himself?

This loving, one-sided guidance constitutes a parental influence or con-trol attempt that is more insidious and thereby much more effective than any declaration of rules and orders can ever be. How and when will the son recognize that, while playing the role of the adventurous explorer with his father, their focus did not include the real world the son was sup-posed to live in some day?

▓ Learning Mastery and Constraint

Childhood is the time to learn that control has at least two components: mastery and constraint. Both are learned in the context of relationships with parents who are more or less loving and beloved. Teenagers believe that they have outgrown their parents and their parents' rules, curfews, and advice. Although teenagers don't mind taking advantage of the room and board their parents provide, as well as their transportation services and money allowances, their personhood is their own, they argue. They should be able to do with their bodies and persons what they want to do without interfering rules from the parents. Parents proclaim that they know what is best for their children, but most children do not buy into that. They believe it is preposterous for their parents to think they know what is relevant to the children's lives: "even when parental controls derive from a caring concern rather than power-tripping or stereotyping, the benevolence of their intentions doesn't make their interference any more palatable. They claim that it's their duty to guide and protect" (Viorst, 1998, p. 82), but the children claim that it's their right to control their own lives.

In their struggles for control children employ various forms of rebellion. They may reject whatever their parents value or they may demand to have now what it took their parents a lifetime to collect. Other forms of rebellion can be seen in covert actions, such as not telling parents what the children are doing, arguing that what parents don't know won't hurt them. Some children may use open defiance, such as "try and make me!" Neglecting chores, not doing homework, keeping their rooms messy, violating curfews, delinquency, drug abuse, and promiscuity are other well-known forms of rebellion. This type of rebellion consumes valuable time and energy that would be more appropriately expanded in the developmental tasks of mastery and constraint.

Reading a recent cry for help in "Annie's Mailbox," a syndicated advice column published in daily newspapers, one can only guess where the process of mastery and constraint went awry, although the results are clearly described. A female reader, "Stressed-Out Stepmom," introduces her problem with a description of her stepson: "Sam is smart, strong, healthy—and lazy" (Mitchell & Sugar, 2009a, p. 32). She goes on to report that Sam dropped out of college, held one job for eight months, and unsuccessfully tried to live at his mother's house. Now apparently, he has moved in with his father and his stepmother, who is upset about Sam's behaviors. He comes and goes as he pleases and spends hours playing video games. The older couple's food bill has doubled due to the new "resident," and they have bought Sam a car in addition to paying for the car's insurance and his cell phone. Understandably, the stepmother is upset, but her husband, Sam's father, tells her she is blowing it all out of proportion.

Although this story is not unique, it presents an interesting view of control dynamics occurring along three lines. Obviously, Sam has not successfully completed the developmental task of mastery and constraint. The birth parents' control strategies in the past apparently laid the foundation for the present relationship between Sam and his father, which shows Sam being in control of his father and stepmother. Although the reason for the divorce of the birth parents is not known, it is not impossible that the father-son relationship affected it in some way. Interestingly, when Sam tried to move in with his mother, her husband demanded that Sam pay rent. It is undisclosed whether or not the mother was in favor of having Sam living with her and her husband. In any event, her husband put down the law for what was acceptable in his home.

Another point of interest is the stepmother's position. From her account it appears that her husband, who had abdicated control to his son, is insisting that she put up with the situation. Where is her influence, what is her power in the situation? In her ploy for advice she stated that she hates to make her husband choose between her and Sam. More importantly, is *she* in a position to choose? Can she say, "Honey, it's either you and I or you and Sam, not the three of us. In fact, your attitude may be an indication that it would be best for me to live by myself." If she is financially or otherwise dependent on her husband, she surrendered control at their wedding.

▓ Personality Patterns and Control

As individuals become targets of control attempts from the environment, they, in turn, devise strategies that are directed at others in order to maintain control over influences from them. We could imagine each individual as a sphere affected by multitudes of incoming and outgoing control vectors. Responses to the various control attempts differ from one person to the next. Some individuals may hardly respond to one type but will strongly react to other types of control efforts, whereas other persons display extreme sensitivity to any and all methods of control by others around them. As the sensitivity to control attempts by others is different for different individuals, the selection of goals and targets employed by the controlling agents also varies from one person to the next. The variety of factors involved in the overall control schemes can make for a rather complicated situation. Seeking explanations for people's behavior, we tend to focus on the constellation of people's personality traits. Insofar as control-related behaviors are expected to be person specific, one can understand them as expressions of different personality types.

Many would agree that the foundations of personality patterns are laid in childhood, as the story reported in the previous section would seem to demonstrate. Interestingly in the newspaper column, Annie's response to the female reader's request for help focused on the damage done to the son, rather than attend to the stepmother's plight.

Based on insecurities people have developed during childhood, three basic personality patterns can be observed in control-exerting individuals (Stenack, 2001). There are the givers, who respond to rejections or lack of acceptance with increased actions of giving, hoping that this will eventually get them what they want: love or acceptance. Another type of control-seeking person is described as the taker: someone shifting from emotional to material values with the attitude, "I'll take what I can get; something is better than nothing." The third type is what the author called the refrigerators. These are people who at some time have been hurt and have decided to shut off their feelings. They have become aloof emotionally in order to protect themselves from further pain. In addition, there are the Okay people, those who decide for themselves, independent of lack of acceptance and attention in childhood.

These categories can be understood as "simply personality models designed to help understand how people act and why . . .[,] people exhibiting certain patterns of behavior. Givers tend to send things, from themselves to others. Takers try to get things from others. Refrigerators stop all exchange. Okays try to keep things in motion between themselves and others" (Stenack, 2001, p. 15). The author cautions that ". . . [no] one is purely reflected in a single category. There are elements of Giver, Taker, and so on in everyone, even very secure people" (p. 15).

On a more complicated level, the five-factor model of personality is a grouping of relatively enduring major trait dimensions that encompass individual differences in motivational, attitudinal, emotional, and interpersonal styles (Digman, 1990). This model of personality organizes personality traits and describes at a global level the dimensions of normal personality: neuroticism (calm–anxious; secure–insecure), extraversion (reclusive–sociable; cautious–adventurous), openness to experience (conventional–original; closed–open), agreeableness (irritable–good natured; uncooperative–helpful), and conscientiousness (undependable–responsible; low–high achievement striving). Thus, each of the five factors represents a continuum of behavior; for example, in the factor conscientiousness, behaviors range from being responsible and dependable to being impulsive and careless.

■ Attachment Styles and Control

From another field of investigation, the area of domestic violence, a remarkable link between personality and attachment styles was suggested (Dutton, 1995a, 1995b; Dutton, Saunders, Starzomski, & Bartholomew, 1994). The investigators' focus was directed mainly on the abusive personality and associated psychological features, such as a fearful attachment style, high scores on a self-report instrument for borderline personality, and elevated scores on chronic anger and trauma symptoms.

Research in this area has led to the development of a four-category theory of adult attachment style, which hypothesizes individuals' internal models of self and others (Tweed & Dutton, 1998). Positive internal models of both self and others are considered to reflect a secure attachment style. Individuals who seek self-acceptance through recognition from others adhere to a preoccupied attachment style; they are continually attempting to get closer and closer in their relationships with others. A dismissing style of attachment seems to be characteristic of people who have a positive internal model of themselves but a negative view of others. Instrumental batterers can be expected in this category, because their abusive actions are not focused exclusively on intimate relationships but are components of general habits. They don't experience the urgency to bond intimately in relationships. The fourth type includes those who have constructed negative internal models of self and others. Their fear of intimacy is expressed in a fearful attachment style.

Insofar as attachment styles have an impact on individuals' feelings about and methods of coping with conflict, a discussion of their influence is relevant here. The processing of conflict situations will likely trigger individuals' feelings connected to their attachment styles. Certain predictions about an individual's responses in conflict situations can be made based on the knowledge of that person's attachment style. Individuals characterized by a fearful attachment style are not only afraid of intimacy, but they also tend to avoid conflict. They usually do what is expected of them, or they are afraid to acknowledge it. Because they have a negative view of others as well as of themselves, they might expect malevolence or punishment from their partners, and they fear rejection.

Individuals with a preoccupied attachment style seem to perceive conflict as a threat to be abandoned. As they concentrate intensely on restoring closeness, they become even more clinging in their behaviors. Dismissing persons, who have a tendency to minimize the importance of the relationship, also minimize the importance of any conflict. They refuse to engage in arguments and avoid conflicts as if they did not exist (Pistole & Arricale, 2003).

In a study examining attachment styles in connection with individuals' feelings about conflict, expressing conflict, and their conflict tactics, the authors analyzed self-report questionnaires from 188 volunteer college students. Their findings indicated that those who endorsed secure attachment reported feeling less threat from arguments than those who admitted to preoccupied or fearful attachment. They were also less concerned with closeness during conflict than those who endorsed preoccupied attachment. The study showed that those with dismissing attachment reported significantly more conflict avoidance than the securely attached. Individuals with secure attachment reported significantly less fighting and more effective arguing than individuals with fearful attachment styles.

Understanding the reasons behind the controlling person's actions does not necessarily give information about what particular goal will restore a sense of security to the controller or how the controller will go about reaching this goal. Some researchers (Tjaden & Thoennes, 2000) have observed a connection between verbally abusive jealous and possessive male partners and future use of physical violence. Thus, nonphysical abuse may be a predictor of physical violence. Indeed, a measure of coercive control behavior seemed to predict severe physical violence later on.

Observing the behaviors and understanding them within the personality dynamics of a particular person in the context of behavior patterns over time would provide additional insight as to the planned consequences to the targeted victim. For instance, behaviors that are normally explained within the category of jealousy, such as an individual's insistence on spending every minute with the other person in the intimate relationship, are often camouflaged as overwhelming love and devotion to the person. Considering the same behaviors within the framework of a preoccupied-fearful attachment style pattern, it becomes a control scheme to limit the personal freedom of the target person.

On the other hand, people with dismissing attachment styles would show less interest in the target than in the goal. The goal might be one of convenience, including such things as being served good meals and having clean laundry and a clean house as well as having sex when wanted. As long as the goal can be obtained, the target person may not have any personal meaning to the controller: the person is a target of opportunity. Considerations of types of control tactics and types of domestic violence situations add more variables to an already complicated picture; however, awareness of the effects of these variables can be of help to potential victims in predicting the danger of their position in the relationship.

Ron held a master's degree in physics. He had considered getting a Ph.D. degree but doubted that the professors at the university could teach him much. Most of his life he had engaged in independent reading. His job was secure and spending his evenings in classes for another degree, just a "piece of paper," seemed like a waste of time. Ron did not have many friends because most people didn't come up to his level of intelligence. His interactions with supervisors and coworkers were brief and superficial.

Although Ron sincerely believed that in general women's level of intelligence was below that of men's, he did get married and admitted that his wife's intelligence was "pretty good for a woman." Ron could be charming and witty, but most of his interactions with others were characterized by sarcasm. He resented it when his wife's friends came to visit; usually he refused to interact with them for more than the briefest of greetings because they were stealing his valuable time. He would not answer the telephone because it was his wife's job to keep intruders away from him. When his sleep became disturbed by some noise, he screamed and yelled at his wife, no matter whether it was in the morning, noon, or in the afternoon—his sleep was sacred. Time spent with his wife was limited to meals and sexual activity directed by him when it suited him. It is safe to say that Ron was successful in keeping others at a distance. He wanted to be in absolute control over his time and with whom and how he spent it. Although not physically abusive to his wife, his constant criticism and blaming amounted to significant emotional abuse. His wife filed for divorce. Surprisingly, it did not take him long to find a replacement.

One might say Ron was practicing a dismissing style of attachment, as described by Tweed and Dutton above. He had a positive self-image—some people would call it an inflated ego—and cared little for those around him.

Because they were of lower intellectual standing, in his mind their functioning was relegated to serving his purposes.

▓ Strivings for Perfection and Control

Considering different personality patterns with regard to controlling behaviors, the characteristic of perfectionism comes to mind readily; it appears to be an almost natural combination. In order to ensure perfect conditions, absolute control over a multitude of influences would be necessary. Although most people would agree that absolute control is impossible to achieve, there are many, who seem intent on accomplishing the impossible. Who cannot relate to perfectionism either by recognizing it in oneself or by knowing someone who is exhibiting signs and symptoms of the condition?

Within the theoretical framework of individual psychology, Alfred Adler (1979) stated as one of the basic assumptions that individuals are striving for success in the solution of their problems although what constitutes success to them varies from individual to individual. In Adler's earlier notions the striving for success included striving for perfection, superiority, or overcoming of deficiencies. The striving for perfection was considered to be an innate characteristic in individuals, something that belongs to life, and life could not be conceived of without it.

Acknowledging the striving for perfection as a fundamental human characteristic, the ways to imagine the goal of perfection and the processes for achieving it differ from one individual to another. Individuals, attempting to reach the goal by dominating others as a demonstration of their own perfection or superiority, are likely to come into conflict with those others in their environment. Likewise, individuals who interpret superiority as leaning on others for their own responsibilities in life might encounter opposition from those targeted for performing those tasks (Adler, 1979).

What are the reasons for people choosing perfectionism as a way of life? Are the answers to be found in genetic factors, does a person's childhood experience play a determining role, or do people just somewhere along the way decide to adopt perfectionism as their philosophy of life?

Various explanations regarding the strivings for perfection have been suggested in the past. An underlying deep sense of insecurity was considered as motivating force for perfectionism (Burns, 1980; Hollender, 1965). In attempting to gain or maintain acceptance from others, perfectionists set unrealistically high goals for themselves that are usually not attainable. While striving for these goals, they are paying the high price of low self-esteem and poor personal relationships (Pacht, 1984; Sorotzkin, 1985).

Perfectionism operates along more than one dimension; it has been conceptualized as a multidimensional construct with both intrapersonal and interpersonal trait dimensions. There is a self-oriented type of perfectionism, which operates along intrapersonal dimensions and requires individuals to be perfect. Individuals set high standards for themselves and use those standards for appraising their own performance. In contrast, other-oriented perfectionism is interpersonal in its application and demands perfection from others. High standards are applied to critically evaluate the performance of others. The third type, the socially prescribed perfectionism, centers on the individual's belief that others hold unrealistic expectations of the individual. The pressure to be perfect in this case comes from society in general (Hewitt & Flett, 1991). High scores on the three categories are considered to be maladaptive and to reflect pathology, but individuals subscribing to these categories to varying degrees are abundant in our society, and they are reflective of the many attempts individuals make to control self and others.

▓ The Control Obsession

Persons who are overly concerned with "everything being in its place" combine elements of self-oriented and other-oriented perfectionist attitudes. In cases where objects or activities in their immediate environment are out of line in some way, they will not rest until what is the perfect order in their mind is restored. Feelings of anxiety and discomfort will not let the individual relax unless everything is in its place. As long as they are living alone, the situation is manageable without significant interpersonal conflicts. However, when sharing living space with others, such as their families, the situation becomes more volatile. Children may forget to place their toys properly in the designated places, or other family members may leave an item of clothing or other personal objects in spaces not assigned for their storage: this is when the other-oriented aspects of perfectionism come into play.

Feeling the strong urge to have everything where it is supposed to be takes on an obsessive-compulsive tendency, which erupts into anger at the sight of items misplaced by others. Forgetfulness or carelessness in removing the dislocated items is interpreted by the control-obsessed individual as a personal affront or misdeed committed on purpose by the other person—just to upset the controller. And even if it had not been an act of malice, but just an overlooked seemingly inconsequential mistake, the negligence is considered to be of such proportions that it represents a blatant act of disrespect for the wishes of the controller.

Bob, a mechanical engineer insisted on having everything exactly lined up in its place. His interactions as supervisor at work followed strict rituals. He never discussed anything in detail at any of his supervisees' workstation; a particular worker would be called into his cubicle that served as an office. As soon as the person followed the direction to sit down, Bob started with his instructions. He paused at certain intervals to hear the worker's questions if he had any. Invariably, Bob determined the end of the meeting. He was the last one to speak, ending with a statement indicating that it was time for the subordinate to return to his workstation. If the worker for whatever reason verbalized his statements and attempted to rise from the chair before Bob had given the dismissal signal, invariably, Bob resumed talking, perhaps about a different issue. The worker could not have the last word. Arriving home from work, Bob changed his clothes, but his behavior remained pretty much the same. There was very little space for spontaneity left in his life.

▓ Fear as Motivator in Control Strivings

Fear, anxiety, or insecurity seem to be a common theme behind control strivings. Although most people incorporate in their personality constellations both strivings toward gaining something of value to them as well as efforts to avoid receiving something unpleasant, avoidance tendencies seem to figure more prominently in the scheme of behavioral motivators. Les Parrott (2000, p. 48) in his book, *The Control Freak*, cites Seneca's statement that the most powerful is the one who has himself in his power, but goes on to say that "[D]eep in the soul of every Control Freak is an ample supply of anxiety, a seemingly endless stream that continually fuels the fear of being out of control. Control Freaks can't relax because they feel at risk of being criticized or shamed for making an error. To feel safe, they feel that they have to be superhuman 24 hours a day. They have to master every situation." The stress arising from the demand for superhuman abilities will eventually wear out the strongest person and render him an equal among the weakest.

What types of situations are high on people's avoidance lists? Physically threatening situations would rank high for many, but then there are the people who actually seek out physically dangerous circumstances because encountering the possibility of injury or death is a thrilling experience to them. They may see themselves as conquering the fear of death and mastering their own survival.

In contrast to fears of being trapped in life-threatening situations, there are various psychological fears that turn people onto the avoidance path. Often the anticipation of experiencing psychological fears greatly outweighs the existence of physical fears in people's minds. What makes psychological fears so potent? As one person said, "If you are in a life-threatening situation and you die, you don't have to face people and worry about what they think of you. But the psychological fears don't kill you—although you wished they would. Being afraid of psychological injury is based on the fact that you remain alive to face humiliation."

Anticipation of harm generates fear or anxiety in most people. What constitutes a fear-inducing situation varies among individuals. The anticipation of harm becomes a function of the subjective likelihood of a harmful outcome state and the severity of that outcome state. For the individual, successful avoidance of a stimulus with harmful potential reduces the probability of experiencing the harmful outcome state to zero. Complete and successful avoidance of fear or anxiety-producing stimuli, however, can only be guaranteed through the ultimate control of every situation the individual is subjected to. Of course, complete control of every circumstance people find themselves in is impossible, but people can *try* for complete control, even if what they are doing is not in their best interest.

Several different fears can relate to the same or similar outcome states anticipated by individuals. For instance, what do the fears of rejection, of hurting someone's feelings, of abandonment, and possibly of confrontation have in common? Most likely, the person is afraid of not being liked by others, perhaps to the point of becoming isolated or abandoned. The fear of confrontation may include additional elements of not being able to defend oneself or one's opinion in arguments with others, which would make the individual appear less intelligent than the opponent in the confrontation. The fear of embarrassment involves similar reasoning. Individuals with those fears most often respond with avoidance of situations where the anticipated harm could materialize. Even those who fear isolation or abandonment may employ avoidance because if they avoid interactions with others, those others cannot abandon them.

Anxieties concerned with possibilities of exploitation and engulfment appear to have a different focus. Rather than fearing a social disadvantage, as in the fears described above, here avoidance behaviors center on experiencing material disadvantages or, as in the case of engulfment, on restrictions of personal freedom or having to assume responsibilities one is not ready for.

▓ Competition and the Fear of Failure

Life for us has become an endless succession of contests. From the moment the alarm clock rings until sleep overtakes us again, from the time we are toddlers until the day we die, we are busy struggling to outdo others. This is our posture at work and at school, on the playing field and back at home. It is the common denominator of American life. (Kohn, 1986, p. 1)

"Competition builds character" or "competition is part of human nature," often heard and repeated assumptions, have found application in the worlds of industry as well as sports. When Roger Smith became chairman of General Motors, one of his stated priorities was to restore the old spirit of competition to the company that dated back to the days of Alfred Sloan. Procter & Gamble had started a policy of brand manager competition back in 1931. Similarly, at Bloomingdale's, merchandising vice presidents, buyers, and fashion coordinators remained in ongoing competition for scarce floor space. Regular reorganizations of the company resulted because of new winners and losers. There are benefits to the internal competition approach, but there are also high costs of duplication, arising from overlapping products and multiple development projects, to say nothing about the general atmosphere within the company (Peters & Waterman, 1982).

Apparently sports psychologists Thomas Tutko and William Bruns considered competition to be a learned phenomenon and suggested that young athletes should be judged only on the basis of their own abilities instead of how they do compared with others (Kohn, 1986). Of course, that is not a reality in the world of sports where, as in politics, only the winners count. Individuals are socialized from early childhood on by schools and often by parents to compete for grades, for trophies, and later on for the highest salaries or the greatest wealth.

If indeed competition were instrumental in building character, what type of character or personality traits would highly competitive people possess and display? A person whose self-esteem depends on always winning or finishing first among others, would have to be constantly alert about seizing every opportunity to get ahead, to be vigilant that no option is left open for others to compete successfully, and to keep others uninformed about any future goals the "competitor" may be considering for the next achievement. If a single area is left uncovered, it may evolve as a breeding ground for failure, a possibility too dreadful to even contemplate. We all have met or heard about such people. They are the ones who have to ensure absolute control over every circumstance they are in. They can never relax; they can never let anyone come close. They have to keep up their guards and their walls around them. If they hurt, nobody is allowed to know it because it could become their Achilles' heel.

▪ The Persistent Personality and Control

In our culture, the word persistence generally carries a favorable connotation. We praise those who have it, and we believe that it is an integral part of being successful. David Lieberman (2000), a psychologist and best-selling author, talks about the power of persistence. He says that people resist change, and therefore, a person asking another for something should not give up after two or three attempts but should continue with the request to the sixth attempt. The author explained that research has shown that six is the magic number and that most people will agree to a request after being asked up to six times.

On the other hand, one could also easily become annoyed at a person who does not take no for an answer, a point the author did not elaborate on. Persistence can be detrimental when carried to the extreme. People who refuse to give up in the face of impossibility and continue their efforts despite an obviously zero probability of goal attainment might find themselves on a course of self-defeating, and often other-defeating, behavior.

Individuals who refuse to accept no for an answer may score initial control points when their refusal to let go is not met with an even stronger expression of rejection. If there is any degree of hesitancy in the response of the pursued, the pursuer most likely will translate this into a "maybe" and step up the control efforts. Occasionally, pursued persons will weaken and tell themselves that it really isn't so bad and that the other person is just strongly committed to the cause. Often the control-seeking individual will test the target person, countering the person's initial hesitancy or resistance with a seemingly inconsequential request or even an offer of assistance, which is designed to make the target person feel at least slightly guilty. Any hesitancy in the target person's behavior at this point is an invitation for the pursuer to continue until a satisfactory degree of control has been established.

In the pursuit of romantic relationships, persistence is often misinterpreted as a sign of love. The more persistent the behavior of the pursuer is the deeper or stronger his or her love for the target person seems to be. Sometimes the target person gains a false sense of security from having the unwavering attention of such a devoted lover; sometimes the target person gives in because the attention appears simply overwhelming—too much to resist. In either case, this is the moment when the target person voluntarily moves into the victim sphere.

▓ A Narrow Escape

Being so ardently pursued by another person can be flattering, and it can increase the pursued person's level of self-esteem. The resulting good feelings may persuade the pursued to stay longer in the controlling relationship than is good for him or her. The longer the pursued person allows him- or herself to bask in the devotion and admiration of the pursuer, the more difficult it becomes to exit the scene.

George, a 37-year-old not-quite-divorced man, had no idea that he was entering the victim sphere when he became romantically involved with Samantha, an attractive 36-year-old business manager. His divorce was expected to become final soon. After several prior separations their final breakup had occurred about a year before. George and his high school sweetheart Elaine had married early; in fact, George had felt pressured into the marriage because Elaine was pregnant. George did what was expected of him. His job entailed a lot of traveling, and Elaine became bored. She embarked upon a few extramarital affairs, which usually did not last long and for which she blamed George. It was his travel, she complained, that caused her to feel lonely. George applied for a position with less travel duties in the company, but it did not work out.

George and Samantha met through mutual friends at a party. There seemed to be an instant chemistry between them—at least, that's how Samantha described it. At the end of the evening Samantha invited George to her home for a drink. He expressed some hesitation but did not want to hurt Samantha's feelings. One drink led to another. When Samantha encouraged him to take off his jacket and loosen his tie, George again hesitated, but Samantha did it for him. Samantha sat close to him on the sofa. With his jacket removed and his tie hanging loose, she unbuttoned his shirt and started to caress his chest. George mentioned that his divorce from Elaine was not final yet and that this seemed like adultery to him. Samantha laughed gently as she explained that as two mature adults they did not have to worry about a little thing like that. Sex felt great—even with the twinge of guilt George experienced at the time. They agreed to meet again in two weeks because the coming weekend George was scheduled for visitation with his children.

Three days after their initial meeting Samantha appeared in the parking lot at George's workplace. She told him she had a surprise for him and asked him to follow her to her home. The surprise was a gourmet dinner Samantha had prepared and that was now ready to be warmed up. Over dinner and wine Samantha explained that she had enjoyed his company so much that she thought two weeks was too long to wait. Sex felt great again. Here was a woman who could not keep her hands off of him. George's self-esteem had been bruised by Elaine's affairs. This seemed like the cure he needed.

The dating process progressed rapidly. Whenever George tried to slow it down, Samantha reassured him that they were ideally suited for one another, so why put their happiness on hold? Not too long after George's divorce had become final, Samantha had another surprise. Her parents had invited them both to spend the Christmas holidays with them at their Florida home. They would have a wonderful time. George was not quite ready to meet Samantha's parents, but he did not want to offend them, and in addition, his children would spend the holidays with their mother anyway, so he accepted the invitation.

Several weeks passed uneventfully before Samantha hinted that their visit to Florida would be a wonderful opportunity to become engaged. When they made love that evening, George had difficulties maintaining an erection. Samantha was understanding and told him he needed rest. His life was so stressful when he had to take care of his children by himself for a whole weekend every other week. No wonder he was worn out; the vacation would do him good. Samantha continued to cook wonderful meals. She even got cookies for him to take home and keep for his children on their visits with him. She listened to his stories about his children and expressed her belief that children were important in a sincere relationship. Sometimes she added that she thought she was ready to settle down soon. Her biological clock was running out.

Samantha was persistent. Whenever George hesitated she gently pulled him back into the net of her control. One day about two weeks before Christmas she handed him two roundtrip plane tickets to Florida; they were a gift from her parents, she explained. George was embarrassed, what could he get as a gift for them? How could he repay their generosity? Samantha had a helpful suggestion; he might find something in a jewelry store. In fact, there was a sale on in a darling little store around the corner from her job. When George did not seem to catch on, Samantha played with the ring she wore on her ring finger. That evening George again had difficulties maintaining his erection. The next day he called a therapist who had been recommended by a friend. He knew he needed help if he were to avoid being pushed into another marriage before being ready for it.

For any prospective target person it would be prudent to understand and remember that persistent behavior that neglects to acknowledge and respect another's wishes is a violation of the person's rights. Compliance with the persistent actions of the pursuer amounts to an agreement to accept the violation of personal rights. What is often mistaken for love and devotion is nothing more than a will to possess, to control, to overpower. The devotion is focused on the controller's obsession for unrestrained power over another. In a similar vein as discussed in later chapters, jealous behavior is not to be mistaken for an expression of love; it is a possessive concern rather than a loving concern for the other person.

Persistence can also be observed in people who are obsessed with their own significance. They often seek affirmation by addressing audiences through speeches, seminars, or other types of presentations. These presentations could be talks on topics that they feel they are experts on, or it could be a report of a journey they took, believing that their experiences in a particular place would be enlightening to others as well. Photographs and slide or movie projections can go on for hours. The skilled presenter will arrange the setting in such a way that he or she has a captive audience, either by making sure that people cannot leave or would be embarrassed to cause hurt feelings by leaving prematurely.

In situations like this, the controlling person's goal is affirmation of personal significance; the target is, of course, the audience, but this is more a target of opportunity than a particular person or persons. As long as the target is a captive audience, other characteristics are not of great importance. This type of controlling behavior, attention seeking, is most often found in individuals with narcissistic personality traits. In their attention-seeking attempts they can be quite persistent, even though the target population may change frequently.

3 ▦ ▦ ▦

A Menu of Control Techniques

Describing all the different control techniques people are devising for themselves would take volumes. This book will highlight and discuss a sampling of different control strategies. Some can be found in the rules and regulations of culture and society; others are developed by individuals in their attempts to cope with life's situations. Individuals can be quite creative in conceiving and executing various ways of establishing and maintaining control or having the upper hand in their interactions with others. The techniques mentioned here are just examples of common approaches that could provide insight for detection of similar but less common strategies. As they are increasing awareness of the various techniques, these examples can also serve as stimulation for modifying the recipient's responses to applied control techniques.

▦ Interaction Rituals: Systems of Society-Sanctioned Control

In social encounters, societies must mobilize their members as self-regulating participants that perform more or less smoothly within accepted boundaries. "One way of mobilizing the individual for this purpose is through ritual; he is taught to be perceptive, to have feelings attached to self and are self expressed through face, to have pride, honor, and dignity, to have considerateness, to have tact and a certain amount of poise. These are some of the elements of behavior which must be built into the person if practical use is to be made of him as an interactant, and it is these elements that are referred to in part when one speaks of universal human nature" (Goffman, 1967, pp. 44–45).

Practically all areas of human activities are subject to rules of conduct. This type of control becomes apparent when we observe the interaction rituals that direct behaviors in formalized settings, such as royal courts, presidential palaces, religious institutions, courts of law, government offices, banking institutions, schools, hospitals, and many others. Rules of conduct govern behaviors among people interacting in these situations. Seating arrangements, dress codes, and arrival times of the participants reflect the levels of control invested in each. Those who are on the higher levels of control have certain expectations regarding the behaviors of those at lower ranks who, in turn, have the obligation to display the expected behaviors.

Thus, what is one man's expectation will often be another's obligation in those interactions. Individuals who carry obligations observe the rules of conduct that regulate and constrain some of their behaviors. Failure to adhere to the rules, whether due to ignorance or to rebellion, can be costly; it can become a matter of shame and humiliation. "In thinking about deference it is common to use as a model the rituals of obeisance, submission, and propitiation that someone under authority gives to someone in authority. Deference comes to be conceived as something a subordinate owes to his superordinate" (Goffman, 1967, p. 58).

The rules of deference incorporate guidelines regulating the extent of personal space of interacting parties. The socially elevated person who expects and receives deference also commands a greater area of personal space than individuals of lower ranks. At corporate executive meetings, the president sits at the head of the table, commanding more personal space than those sitting alongside the table. The ritual proceeds silently. Without being told, every person entering the room will avoid taking the seat at the head of the table unless that person is the president. The furniture arrangement in the room—whether it includes a round, a square, a rectangular, or an oval table occupying the middle of the room—spells out the rules of conduct for the particular situation.

Along with folklore and myth, rituals function as powerful forces in shaping meanings and transmitting elements of our culture. As symbolic enactments, rituals express the community's worldview to its members. Rituals perpetuate certain "truths" and maintain particular vested interests. Life experiences are organized into particular patterns of interactions. Communal rituals can bind individuals to common goals and strategies, thereby minimizing differences but also blinding the group members to alternative ways of doing and living (Laird, 1991).

Rituals also function in supporting beliefs that we hold and never question. When we don't question beliefs, it is relatively easy to lose sight of the reasons for their existence. Rituals perform a confirmatory action, which eliminates the need for challenging beliefs and confronting them with reality. During their upbringing, individuals will be instilled with sets of beliefs that can easily masquerade as knowledge if adopted unquestioningly. Most often this occurs when the individual is too young to be discerning regarding the validity of the beliefs. The combined effect of childhood indoctrination and the messages inherent in the socialization process, strengthened by the use of rituals, can lead individuals to blind themselves to reality and to depend on a given belief system as if, indeed, it were knowledge. Participation in and repetition of actions help to confirm one's conviction in the validity of the belief. What better methods for coaching and programming can we find than the use of rituals?

The pervasive nature of rituals in situations of daily living provides directives and suggestions for the individual application of control techniques sanctioned by a given society. Language is such an area as it includes guidelines for speech patterns between persons of higher and lower ranks or social positions; it can be easily adapted to individual communication patterns between male and female participants.

▓ Language and Speech Patterns as Control Techniques

Considering language use as a social strategy, one can conceive of different categories for using language in order to make people do or say things as well as to get and keep their attention for the maintenance of social relationships with the speaker (Guerin, 2003). When trying to influence people to say something, the goal is usually the target person's verbal agreement with the speaker. In the case of influencing a person to do something, however, the expectations involve actual behaviors that are of benefit to the speaker. When language is used to gain someone's attention, the enhancement of the speaker's status or social standing is likely the goal. Enhanced social standing also is a consequence of successfully using language in order to have others remain in relationships with the speaker, but this strategy can result in broader benefits as well, such as may arise from being liked by others.

Thus, language in the shape of discourse can function as a form of domination. The use of speech expresses an index of social values and the distribution of power within a society (Thorne, Kramarae, & Henley, 1983). Participants in verbal interactions exercise and maintain power by employing various tactics. Usually, persons who want to maintain control disclose very little about themselves during verbal exchanges, believing that such disclosure of a personal nature can be used against them.

What can turn language into such a valuable tool is its predictability. Verbal interactions follow certain pathways, whether or not the speakers are actually aware of it. A given statement will trigger a relatively small variety of responses. With a little bit of knowledge of the listener's personality his or her responses can be predicted by the speaker. For instance, an individual with a generally defensive attitude will likely respond in a defensive way to an inquiry about why a task has not been performed. If the person is defensive but shy or easily intimidated, the defense most likely will be uttered in a soft voice without aggressive undertones. If, however, the person's defensive attitude also includes some angry or belligerent components, the defense will likely be accompanied by a counterattack, such as an accusation, guaranteed to spiral the verbal exchange into an argument. In the "heat" of an argument it becomes easy to break up relationships; for example, provoking a lover one would like to leave into an angry verbal exchange containing words one just cannot forgive or forget.

Another version of control is displayed in the responses individuals give to topics introduced by another person. One-syllable responses are expressions of disinterest in the topic under discussion, indicating that the topic is not an issue of significance and does not warrant much attention. The extreme form of this control technique in conversation is silence. Nothing kills a topic of discussion faster and defeats the speaker's credibility more effectively than absolute silence from the listener. Silence here is not merely the absence of words; silence speaks louder than any words can do.

In discussions, speaking in an inexpressive manner often conveys the notion of control or what Sarah Myers McGinty (2001), an expert in the field of linguistics, called the affect of control. Elements characterizing the affect of control include the speaker's straight posture, looking directly at the audience, controlled facial expressions, and brevity of speech (p. 29): "[L]anguage style is another public power marker." Pronouncing decisions or suggestions in an impersonal and inexpressive way lends an aura of autonomy and "correctness" to the speaker's position because his or her verbalizations appear to be conclusions arrived at through pure logic and unemotional rationality.

Yet another control method observed in verbal exchanges involves the number and frequency of interruptions by the "listener." Interruptions express a low level of interest for the topic as well as a lack of respect for the person who initiated the topic. When Pamela Fishman (1983) analyzed patterns of conversation in households of heterosexual couples, she found that women were more often responsible for initiating a conversation than men, but they succeeded less often because of the minimal responses they received from their male companions. On the other hand, when men raised topics, the women asked more questions and demonstrated more support than the men did in their minimal responses to topics introduced by women. The author drew the conclusion that the women produced the most work, but the men controlled the conversations.

The author's conclusion can be understood within the context that speech strategies of men and women emerge from their structured positions of inequality. The strategies used by men to exercise and maintain control over women in conversations include limited response to the topics raised by women, interrupting women more than women interrupt men, and withholding self-disclosure. Women, on the other hand, contribute to their lower position by listening to men's speech attentively and by expressing approval and interest with questions and comments at appropriate times.

Within the context of structured positions of inequality, the power of gender still outweighs position in some people's minds (Fishman, 1983). When a group of female judges was asked about their experiences with control issues in the courtrooms, one of the female judges responded with "some of the male attorneys are the worst manipulators that ever entered the halls of justice." She elaborated on her statement by explaining how some male attorneys while pleading their case in front of female judges make it a point to address them by their first names, accompanied by a smile that expresses an inappropriate familiarity. The reason for this breech of professional behavior is seen as a combination of wanting to control the judge's attitude in the case and to impress their clients of their influential position with the judge. It usually takes a summons for the attorney to approach the bench to remind him of his unethical behavior to make him stop his control attempts, the judge continued. Although even after uttering a feeble excuse, some attorneys don't give up at the first reprimand.

Eye contact is an adjunct to control techniques that are exercised in speech. Victoria Valian (1998) described how people of higher rank look at their subordinates while speaking, but when listening to those of lower rank their gaze is not fixed intently on the speaker's face. By contrast, subordinates look at their superiors more when listening to those of higher rank than when speaking to them: "Looking at the other person carries a different message, depending on whether one is speaking or listening. Looking expresses power when you are talking; you are actively soliciting the other person's attention. Looking expresses deference when you are listening. You look at the other person to assure her or him that you are paying attention" (p. 149).

Another path for verbal control can be opened with the use of questions. Asking questions strengthens the possibility of at least a minimal response. In attempts to ensure a basic level of interaction, women generally seem to ask more questions than men do. However, questions like "Why did you decide not to come to the meeting?" take on an interrogative quality, and this type of question is more frequently used by men. The person questioned may fall into the trap of believing that after the questioner knows the reasons for the absence, he will understand and agree, when actually the use of the "why" question affords the questioner the opportunity to belittle the other person twice: first for the actions and then again for faulty reasoning.

Using questions in rapid succession, especially when dealing with the same subject matter, can transmit the notion that the person answering the questions did not do so with sufficient clarity to be understood. The use of this questioning technique serves two functions. First, it interrupts the speaker, similar to the interruptions mentioned earlier. In addition, when after a sufficient interval the questioner finally gives up pursuing the topic, this method points to the speaker's lack of competence, implying that the speaker is unable to use comprehensible thought and expression regarding the topic under discussion.

In business meetings or conference presentations one can often observe the successful application of this technique by those who attempt to discredit a particular speaker. A final question in the quizzical process might be verbalized as follows: "Are you familiar with Dr. XYZ's recent groundbreaking findings on this subject?" The speaker's apology to the effect that he or she is not familiar with the information in question becomes the victory for the controlling audience member. Obviously, there is no further need for discussion of the topic because the speaker is not in possession of the latest information on the topic he or she is talking about.

Other types of questions, such as, "You are going to iron my shirt before I leave for work, aren't you?" are actually demands couched in the form of questions, graciously leaving the other person with the opportunity to confirm that, indeed, this will be taken care of to the satisfaction of the controlling person. The question form is designed to make the controlling person sound as though he is asking rather than giving orders, but also implying that any sensible human being would perform the requested activities. Furthermore, it gives the appearance that the target person has a choice of whether or not to perform the chore. Thus, it appears as if the persons carrying out the task do so of their own free will and because it is the sensible thing to do. The controlling person would be hard pressed to admit that questions like those are attempts to exercise control over others.

A seemingly more gentle control approach is seen in persuasion, a topic that will be discussed in a later chapter dealing with marketing for control in politics and advertising. Nevertheless, there are also opportunities in interpersonal interactions for this type of persuasive controlling. Picture for example, a professional meeting, hosted by an agency publicizing new services. The audience in this type of meeting consists of professionals who might use the services and those who might want to function as adjuncts performing the services as well as those who regard this as an opportunity to persuade those around to give them a piece of the action. The fact that people wear nametags at this type of meeting is clearly of benefit.

Professional A can be observed entering the room, picking up his name-tag, and scanning the participants. He discovers one person, professional B, with a slightly familiar name seated at a table with several other professionals who seem to be part of employee assistance networks. Person A approaches B with an elaborate greeting and proceeds to praise B's achievements to the highest levels imaginable. B is gracious enough to listen and thank A for the compliments, although some of it seems exaggerated. Meanwhile professional A turns to the others at the table, introduces himself, dispersing his business cards while continuing to sing B's praise to them. He places himself between professional B and the other persons, maintaining direct communication with the employee assistance professionals while practically isolating B.

What are professional A's gains in this scenario? He has efficiently isolated professional B without offending him or anybody else. He has portrayed himself as a congenial and trustworthy individual who personally knows distinguished experts in his field (although professional B is not nearly as accomplished as A indicated, but that does not mater to A, who does not know B well anyway). By praising B to such high levels, he practically placed him out of competition for any referrals from the employee assistance people because they are not looking for famous but rather for affordable professionals to send their employees to. Professional A's seemingly compassionate and noncompetitive attitude as well as being knowledgeable of other professionals' work persuaded the target persons (employee assistance professionals) that A was the perfect referral choice for them.

Although professional B realized at this point how he had become a victim of A's persuasive techniques, there was not much he could do at this particular occasion. However, professional B would do well to remember and prepare himself for professional A's strategies in future meetings. Instead of listening to the praise, B might point out that professional A must be mistaking him for someone else. Carefully played out, this approach could function to isolate A from the rest of the group.

Temper Tantrums, Emotional Blackmail

Temper tantrums usually are displays of anger or rage. When not getting what they want, people may throw things, raise their voices, and even imply the threat of physical harm to others. An interesting scenario can be observed when the anger-expressing person blames the other for the anger outburst: "It's your fault that I lost control; you made me so angry." Here the controlling person blames the angry or violent action on behaviors of the other person. Usually we describe the person throwing a temper tantrum as being "out of control"; however, rather than being out of control, the person might actually be engaging in purposeful behavior, pursuing the goal of getting what he or she wants. As long as the target person is duly impressed and gives in to the demands of the temper tantrum, it works; the temper tantrum has established a parameter of control to some extent.

There is, however, another side to the anger issue. Angry individuals can be controlled by those who have observed them closely and intend to handicap the angry persons by triggering in them those strong negative emotions. Once these emotions are in operation, they successfully distract the angry person from the controller's purpose and intentions. Learning about the truly angry person's "anger buttons" enables the controller to sidetrack angry individuals from their goals by pushing those buttons and rendering them—for the moment—helpless targets.

Another form of temper tantrums, suicide threats or gestures, functions as an example of emotional blackmail, "If you don't do what I want, I will kill myself" or "I can't live without you," implying suicidal ideation if the other person should think of leaving. Milder forms of emotional blackmail can be seen in the following argument: "You should do what I tell you to because I know what's right. When you are not following my suggestions [demands], it shows me that you don't trust me. If you loved me, you would trust me. Therefore, your lack of trust means that you don't really love me. That makes me love you less, or makes me feel depressed and disappointed."

In some interactions, control attempts are disguised as requests for love. Statements like, "If you loved me, you would be more involved in my interests; you would share my hobbies" or "If you loved me, you would understand me and know what I need without my telling you so." Does love demand understanding, mind reading, and sharing activities, or can love exist in acceptance despite not fully understanding the other? Love tied to demands is not an unconditional love; it implies we cannot love the other for the person he or she is. If we can only love a person for the similarity to ourselves, is that not just another instance of self-love, such as, in loving you I really love myself?

Other controlling behavior disguised as love-based concern can be found in attempts where one person will not allow the other to venture out alone. For instance, the husband who tries to keep his wife at home by saying, "I don't want you to go out by yourself at night; it's too dangerous," which may appear protective of his wife's safety. However, so long as he does not offer to accompany her to and from her destination so that she can enjoy her evening out, it can be assumed that his statements are based on possessiveness rather than love. This type of control attempt was described by a reader's request for advice in the popular Ann Landers column: "Response to 'Living Dangerously in Ohio:'" "I was married to 'Judd' for 12 years. At first I was flattered by his extreme jealousy and possessiveness. Later, he became controlling and verbally abusive. . . . I was not allowed to go anywhere without him, including the grocery store. He had to approve of my phone calls" (Landers, 2002, p. 5B). The reader's complaint is illuminating insofar as she discloses that she misinterpreted and neglected the early danger signals sent out by her husband. Instead of recognizing his early control attempts, she was flattered by them.

Whatever the excuse for controlling behaviors, it is not to be confused with love or devotion. The two have nothing in common. Adult controlling behavior is self-centered or possessive in nature and is concerned only with the welfare of the person who displays the controlling behavior, whereas loving behavior takes the welfare of the other, the loved one, into consideration.

Both verbal and nonverbal expressions have a potential for influencing relationships by changing the relative status of the partners and the pattern of their interactions. Expressions of fear and sadness may signal vulnerability but may also be an attempt to elicit compassion and assistance from the other, whereas expressions of anger may pretend to signal strength or assertion of independence while they also function to threaten or intimidate the other person. Additionally, expressions of anger can be interpreted as signs of vulnerability because the angry person apparently does not get what he or she wants. Vulnerability is also announced by the person expressing strong distress, which can be an invitation to being taken advantage of by others.

As expressions of emotions are sources of information about an individual's internal state as well as his or her relationship with the environment, these expressions can work in adaptive or maladaptive ways (Kennedy-Moore & Watson, 2001) and, sadly, they can be used to turn individuals into targets by those who intend to control them. In other words, what might have been adopted as coping devices in dealing with distress can be recognized as signs announcing vulnerability.

The "helpless victim" behavior is a type of controlling behavior that is less obvious on the surface and therefore more difficult to detect. This type of person appears unable to cope with various situations, ranging from adhering to a diet to handling surprise visits from a mother-in-law. He or she is railroaded into making unintentional promises, followed by indulging in procrastination. The victim's tales usually elicit sympathy and well-meant suggestions from the listener. However, whatever solution is recommended by the would-be rescuer, the victim counters with "Yes, that sounds good, *but* I tried that and it did not work." The list of "Yes buts" is at least as long as the list of proposed solutions offered by the listener. With this strategy the person who offered helpful suggestions is made to feel incompetent; everything the person can think of has been tried already and proven to be useless. Thus, the apparent victim remains in control of the interaction. For the seemingly helpless person it is a game of one-upmanship, and for the helper it becomes a fruitless exercise in trying to provide possible solutions, followed by frustration, until the helper decides to end the frustration by exiting the relationship.

▦ Ingratiating Behaviors

Ingratiating behaviors comprise yet another promising path for control. Whether it is the person who always grabs the check at the restaurant or the one who bestows gifts upon others that the recipients find difficult to reciprocate in an equal manner, targets of these actions usually feel helpless. Far from the gratitude experienced in appropriate gift giving, the recipients feel obligated and in the giver's service, until finally equality is reached to restore the emotional equilibrium between the parties.

However, a balanced status is what the skillful "ingratiator" works hard to avoid. A person using this method of control wants to be able to "collect" rewards at a time determined by the controller that often is inconvenient to the controlled. It does not matter if the occasion is inopportune; the victim is called on to repay the outstanding debt. The ingratiator would agree with La Rochefoucauld's saying, "Too great haste in paying off an obligation is a kind of ingratitude" (quoted in Beck, 1968, p. 355; from *Reflections*, 1678, 226).

Similar dynamics operate in situations with those who can always be counted on to help: friends and relatives, who do not seem to have any significant activities planned, except for their jobs; who don't have schedules that can't be changed, appointments that can't be broken, or trips that can't be postponed when friends are in need. Because they are so readily available with their assistance, they get called on frequently. Why bother asking someone else who might be busy when "Helpful Harvey" can be counted on to jump in?

Harvey, who gave himself the nickname, had learned it from his mother. His mother was a martyr. Whenever a favor was asked of her, she would do what was requested, even if it was inconvenient for her. She sacrificed much of her life's energies for the sake of the principles "What goes around, comes around" or "Kindness begets kindness," as she would tell Harvey. "People owe you, and they will like you and want you around." Although Harvey remembered his mother complaining at times about how people seemed to forget what she had done for them, he followed her guidance. Harvey did not feel special in any way; in fact, his self-confidence was rather low. He was not particularly good-looking but not ugly either. He was of about average intelligence, but was rather quiet. When he was young, girls did not find him exciting, and that did not change with age; thus, he remained a bachelor. In his occupation he did a good job and could be counted on to work overtime on a short notice. Harvey was a wonderful uncle to his siblings' and friends' children, and he could be relied on to help with family gatherings.

Unlike the ingratiators described above who don't miss an opportunity to collect, people like Harvey and his mother operate on the principle of reciprocity, doing a favor for somebody who then—as the ingratiator hopes—feels obligated to return the favor. In business this technique often takes the form of giving free samples; cult members have used this technique in handing flowers to people on the street to get their attention and good will (Cialdini, 1993). On an individual basis, the "Helpful Harvey"-type ingratiators do what they are asked to do with the hope of ingratiating themselves, but they suffer quietly when their hopes are not fulfilled. They don't dare request repayment openly and directly; they wait and wait silently, building up mountains of disappointment and resentment. They are aware of the fact that other people in their environment do much less to help and are expected less to make themselves available in times of need, yet they are equally welcome at social gatherings.

However, the "Helpful Harveys" continue in their ways because they firmly believe that if they denied a favor, people would not like them and would avoid their company altogether. They still assume that their control attempts work (and wanting to control is what motivates their behavior) because their family and friends have not discarded them as yet. Though the price they pay for their acceptance increases from year to year, they passively but firmly hold onto their illusions of control.

A recent contribution to Annie's Mailbox, a newspaper advice column, could have come from Helpful Harvey's mother. "Sad at Christmas" wrote that she had "for many years been the one who arranges Christmas for my extended family. I make sure the tree is decorated, that everyone receives a present and that the grown kids remember to give gifts to their relatives. Every year, I receive less help and fewer gifts. Last year, I found myself sitting among family members who had piles of boxes in front of them, and I had nothing. When they saw I had no gifts, they all claimed they were too busy and assumed someone else would have given me something" (Mitchell & Sugar, 2009b).

It could be argued that "Sad at Christmas" is just concerned with preserving the Christmas spirit for her family, but it could also be that she wants to make sure that everyone comes to her home for Christmas, so that she will not be alone. Although she is willing to work for that, she also noticed that her efforts lose importance to the family members. As she stated, she receives less help and fewer presents. Just like Harvey and his mother, though, despite dwindling returns on her investment, she continues with her efforts. Her reminders to the grown kids were not powerful enough to include her as one of their relatives. Finally, she had to face the fact that nobody took the time to think about her and her expectations of a gift.

Her request for advice came during the month before yet another Christmas. Was she wondering how to increase her control efforts in order to have the family members visit with her on Christmas? Was she hoping that a family member would read the advice column and, recognizing the person behind Sad at Christmas would feel sufficiently guilty? Or will she accept the fact that her control efforts are not working for her?

Codependency, a term much used in the field of chemical dependency, describes behaviors of friends and family members of the substance-abusing identified client as they enable the addicted or abusing clients to continue with their self-defeating lifestyles. On the surface, it would seem contradictory to ascribe controlling behaviors to a codependent individual. However, Melody Beattie's (1992, p. 36) definition reveals the true underlying dynamics operating in the situation: "A codependent person is one who has let another person's behavior affect him or her, and who is obsessed with controlling that person's behavior." In many ways, the self-defeating behavior of the substance-abusing person becomes as important to the codependent person as it is to the abusing or substance-dependent person.

An interesting parallel to controlling behaviors was drawn by authors who discussed the occurrence of what they called "emotional vampirism" (Rhodes & Rhodes, 1998). Emotional vampirism describes types of predatory behaviors that are often unrecognized by others and that fall outside the limits of officially punishable behaviors. Persons who engage in the behaviors are thought to crave more emotional energy than they can generate on their own. The goal is seen as draining their victims of energy in order to empower or energize themselves. These energy-stealing behaviors can be demonstrated as a desire for attention or control, as passive-aggressiveness, as manipulation, or as simple rudeness. For the victim, the consequences of the predator's goal-directed behaviors range from fatigue or impaired concentration that may result in discomfort from minor harassment to serious psychological injury to their careers and personal lives. Emotional vampires' strongest survival skill is secrecy; they operate in a psychological haze filled with euphemisms, double-speak, and half-truths. In long-term, close relationships, emotional vampirism often contains a large gray area of mesmerized victim consent.

Insofar as the emotional vampire has been described as self-centered, cunning, and compulsively seeking the excitement of emotional turmoil, the victims are often targets of opportunity rather than prespecified persons who may have caused the vampire anger or distress. Whoever is available to fill the needs is acceptable to the vampire. What makes the emotional vampires successful is their victims' susceptibility to the aura of excitement surrounding the vampire—at least, in the beginning. As they get sucked into the process, they might even volunteer for tasks needed to keep the excitement level up, only to sink down in exhaustion when they have depleted their energy reservoirs. In the meantime, the emotional vampire has gained new lifeblood to approach the next target. Successful group leaders incorporate some characteristics of the emotional vampire as they keep the enthusiasm of their group members going to accomplish the projects they set out for.

▓ The Goals behind Control Techniques

In relationships control is not a one-dimensional force or a one-way street; the other person can and does exert control, too. How to handle this most effectively is worth exploring. One of the first steps in dealing with control issues in relationships is the recognition of the goals each of the controlling players is seeking to achieve. Because all behavior is purposeful, controlling behavior can be assumed to serve a purpose or to have a goal. As presented in Chapter 1, the goal may be to attain something of value or to avoid receiving something feared. Sometimes the individual's personality characteristics can contain clues as to whether a given person acts predominantly out of an avoidance or an attainment framework.

Limited emotional accessibility is a technique that operates within the framework of limited commitments. The person who generally tends to avoid complete involvement or complete disclosure of feelings or intentions defines and exercises the limits of availability. Underlying reasons for this approach can be seen as defense or protection measures, such as guarding an innermost part of the person's feelings and thinking from disclosure to others. Keeping others at a distance is the function of this approach, and it can be enacted whenever it seems desirable to the person.

Thus, the goal of limited emotional accessibility may be to preserve a level of personal freedom within the parameters of expressed commitments. While physically present, the person may be emotionally inaccessible. At times, the emotional distancing can serve as a transition to include physical distancing as well. In such situations involving emotional or physical withdrawal, explanations are seldom offered. The person may just quietly fade out emotionally or physically, perhaps uttering a brief statement at the physical departure.

Targets, those persons around people practicing limited emotional accessibility, are usually taken by surprise when the withdrawals occur; they may not even think of questions to ask at the time. Perhaps later they will wonder, "Why did the person not respond to my feelings?" Or "Did I do or say something to upset the person?" After an initial vague feeling of discomfort at the avoidance tactics, others may get the impression of having been manipulated into being left hanging without a resolution. This method of control works especially well with people who experience fears of abandonment and who suffer from anxiety and frustration when they are left dangling without having "closure" of the situation. Although those target persons who believe that they need closure will try to exert their own type of control by pushing toward closure to relieve their frustration, the control expert thwarts their efforts by withdrawing further.

Other subtle methods of control may operate within the framework of unspecified commitments. Most people who are bound in commitments have entered them sincerely and are taking them seriously, but the promises "for better or for worse" or "until death do us part" cover a wide area and seem limitless, except for the death of one of the commitment partners. When the parameters of commitments are not specified, they can be stretched to include all kinds of control strategies. That is precisely the goal of those who suggest or invite others to participate in ambiguous and limitless commitments. In unspecified commitments, these control attempts are often difficult to recognize because of their vague nature and the many possible facets inherent in poorly defined situations.

Consider for instance the story of Rita and Rick, a young couple on their way to a promising future (Maass, 2002/2006). Both were involved in careers of their choice. Shortly before their wedding, Rita discovered that she was pregnant. Although both had agreed on having children, Rick considered it to be a near-disaster at this time in their lives. A few years later would be the appropriate time for starting a family. Rita resisted the thought of having an abortion, but Rick reminded her that they both had made commitments to each other to be helpmates and to make each other happy. At the time when they made the commitment, they did not perceive a need to specify the terms of the commitment more clearly. However, it would never have occurred to Rita that an abortion could be part of the commitment. She, however, decided to honor the commitment in the terms that Rick seemed to have meant them and had the abortion. Although the commitment was honored, the marriage did not survive beyond a few years after that.

One of the most frequently observable control methods is that of criticizing. The underlying dynamics of this technique can be understood as a defense mechanism with the goal of avoiding attacks from others. True to the motto "offense is the best defense" the person seeking control attacks others before they can criticize or attack. It does not really matter whether or not others intend to attack; the attack-defense mechanism has been firmly established and can take on a life of its own at any moment. Criticizing or attacking others keeps them at a distance and busy with defensive movements without leaving them any time or energy to strike back at the attacker. While the attacked individual is busy defending, the attacker is safe from criticism directed at him or her.

Mildred, a middle-aged office worker, was most accomplished in the use of this type of control. Her searching eyes found her mostly female coworkers' imperfections. Ladies' blouses and jackets made of knit fabric often show the dents made by clothes hangers as they are stored in their owners' closets. As soon as she spotted such dents, Mildred triumphantly announced her discovery, "Jennifer, you forgot to take out the hanger before you put on your jacket." This attack worked perfectly insofar as Jennifer would be afraid of ever pointing to any of Mildred's shortcomings because Mildred in return would most likely double her attacks on Jennifer. Furthermore, any of her colleagues witnessing Mildred's harassment of Jennifer were warned to treat Mildred with caution—just what Mildred had intended to happen.

Accomplished criticizers like Mildred will seize every opportunity to practice and apply their control skills; any person in their environment serves as a welcome target. Others in their environment may come to fear them, which is the goal of the attacker because the fear will prevent or inhibit any criticism from others, until they finally come to recognize what is happening to them and how they are being manipulated. At that point of awakening the target persons may prepare for a speedy escape if possible or remain on the periphery, refusing to participate in the contest.

Similar dynamics operate in the presence of the person who uses questioning or interrogating as control techniques, as mentioned earlier. Recipients of this technique find themselves busy answering questions and defending or justifying their actions without having enough breath and energy left to turn the tables and question the motives of the controller or to express their own wishes. Keeping the target person busy with providing answers and defending actions or opinions renders the person harmless to the attacker—at least for the moment.

Repeated bombardments with questions function in ways similar to the criticizing technique; the victim will be unable to confront the attacker and will eventually develop a fear of the controlling person. Thus, both techniques serve similar purposes and address similar goals.

In the example used earlier about questioning someone regarding absence from a scheduled meeting, the questioner's goal in asking, "Why did you decide not to come to the meeting?" was not to learn the person's reasons for the absence. The main goal was to administer criticism and punishment. Furthermore, by the choice of the words "why did you *decide*" the questioner implied that there were no reasons as compelling as a natural catastrophe that could have kept the person from attending the meeting. It was merely the person's decision—perhaps made on the basis of a whim and certainly not important enough to excuse the person's absence from the meeting.

Similarly, the goal behind a question, "Why didn't you have dinner ready when I came home?" is not to explore the reasons behind the missing dinner, although the target person, most likely the wife, will defend herself with a list of reasons. If the questioner had been concerned mainly with dinner, he might have asked, "What food do we have in the house that we can eat now?" The target person, after realizing that the question's goal was to criticize her for her shortcomings or her low level of love and care, rather than a genuine concern about an empty stomach, could have saved herself from reciting her list of reasons and instead could have used her energies for arriving at a more self-enhancing response.

Likewise, the real goal of Harvey's helpful behaviors was not just to assist his friends in time of need. He wanted to be accepted and included in their activities because he felt unimportant and lonely without them. Perhaps we can also understand part of his goal as avoidance of assuming responsibility for building a meaningful and rewarding life of his own. Instead he resigned himself to existing on the fringes of his friends' lives.

Regardless of whether the goal lies in obtaining an advantage or avoiding suffering a disadvantage, once the control methods become obvious through observation, this information can be used by others to thwart the individual's efforts and thus, in turn, control the individual. In other words, information about a person's underlying reasons for and methods of controlling the environment can be turned around and become instruments of control in the hands of astute observers. Both types of control schemes usually include elements of discomfort or pain for self or others.

■ Discovering the Goals in Applied Control Techniques

Sometimes the goals of control-seeking individuals are obvious; at other times what appears to be the goal is merely a minor target along the controller's path, as discussed earlier. What does the controller really want? Could observers of the control-seeking person's behaviors differentiate between the real objective and the minor hurdles along the way?

Individuals attempting to control various aspects of their work environment often leave behavioral clues that are easily interpreted. Friendly and helpful behaviors toward coworkers, especially when supervisors are near, can be explained with wanting to be seen as a "team player" and to impress others as willing to jump in when help is needed to finish a project. The same individuals, staying around after work or arriving early—depending on the likelihood of the chief's presence—performing activities that are designed to attract the boss's benevolent attention, can be thought of as wanting to make a personal impact beyond just being another face in the crowd of employees. When adding the two behavior paths into one control approach, it is not difficult to arrive at the conclusion that the real goal is competition with coworkers for a promotion.

It might take longer to detect the main objective in situations where individuals compliment others on their skills and talents or their initiative or cleverness in finding the best bargains, thereby endearing themselves to others. On the surface it appears that those individuals want to be liked by others or to receive others' sympathy for being less skilled, less clever, or less competent than those they so openly admire or envy. Probing below the surface, it might become apparent that the real goal is to have others do their work for them, run their errands for them, and generally to press others into service for themselves. After all, why take the time to shop around for bargains when others seem to know already where to get them? They might as well get the bargains for their helpless friends too. The smiles and endearing demeanor serve to make the real goal less obvious—at least in the beginning.

The "endearment" approach plays on the good will of others to help those less fortunate or less competent, whereas the "ingratiating" approach mentioned earlier has its roots in feelings of guilt inspired in the target person by the calculating generosity of the controller. Unlike the passively suffering martyr, the actively ingratiating controller usually schedules the "collection" time and there is little doubt left that the victim is expected to pay up. If the payment does not meet the controller's expectations, an increase in guilt feelings is sure to plague the prey.

How often does the cycle have to be repeated before the target person learns the lesson? For some it takes many repetitions—and often with a wide variety of "controllers" because the target person has developed a response set that is as well established and as well practiced as the repertoire of techniques used by the controller. Relying on habituated responses may prevent the target person from discovering the actual goals, and without that knowledge there is little opportunity to influence the outcome or consequences of the control scheme.

A person X might seek out certain people, attempting to establish friendly relationships with them. Again, on the surface it would seem that this individual is longing for the company of certain others. "Perhaps he feels lonely" could be an explanation. Only later when the person makes derogatory remarks about another person Y, who seems to be acquainted with all those people that person X has become friendly with, may the real objective, revenge on person Y, become known.

Call waiting, a service developed by the telephone company, functions as a wonderful control tool to accommodate a variety of goals. Perhaps the individual subscribing to the service is concerned about missing important phone contacts while the line is tied up with another phone conversation. However, a different goal is intended by the young woman who presents her mother with call waiting as a Mother's Day gift. The daughter wants to make sure that her mother pays attention whenever she wants to talk to her. The "gift" allows the daughter to essentially control her mother's attention to others by interrupting conversations at will. People at the other end of the phone conversation will often become frustrated by those interruptions and will eventually reduce or eliminate their calls to those who subscribe to call waiting. The attention-seeking daughter thus becomes instrumental in her mother's growing isolation from others. Of course, the ultimate beneficiary is the telephone company, which provides this "service" for a price.

Telephone services happily provide opportunities for control to the general public. As one reader complained to Miss Manners (Martin, 2009b): In the past, long-distance telephone calls from friends were appreciated as ways of staying in touch with them. However, as the reader observed, with the existence of mobile phones, long-distance calls have become much more frequent and more intrusive. The reason for that change can be found in the fact that by making calls to a mobile phone the receiver is being charged for the cost of the telephone call. Where in the past people may have thought twice before dialing a long-distance number, now the cost for the call will be charged to the phone bill of the receiver, who is not in a position to reject the call. Owners of mobile phones have two choices: either disconnect fast when they don't want to talk long distance or—even better—keep the number of their mobile phone a secret.

For those who believe that they are targets of controlling behaviors from others around them, discovering for themselves the goals most likely pursued by the controller is a first step in protecting themselves. Keeping in mind that every action has a purpose and every behavior has a goal, one can detect and predict the steps along the path of the control-seeking person because "the truth is that every thought is preceded by a perception, every impulse is preceded by a thought, every action is preceded by an impulse, and man is not so private a being that his behavior is unseen, his patterns undetectable" (de Becker, 1997, p. 16).

▦ Misguided Control Techniques

In reality, any control technique can be effective or ineffective, depending on the alertness and willingness of the intended target person. Most situations include several points at which the target person can discern the particular control techniques applied by the controlling person. The target person then has opportunities to impact the consequences of the interaction. In situations of "why" questions discussed above, the target person only needs to supply one explanation regarding the reasons why something was done or not done. If the controller's next statement circumvents this explanation by asking another why question or by supplying a criticizing statement, the target person is able to detect that the actual reason for the incident was not the controller's main interest; criticizing the target person was the real goal. The list of misguided control techniques is long and varied.

Whimpering or talking inaudibly while crying—behaviors meant to evoke sympathy or even pity in the other person—often miss the target or even backfire because the target person experiences difficulty listening to and understanding the words in that approach. Instead of sympathy, the listener may experience a sense of boredom or frustration and may leave the scene either physically or emotionally. The whimpering behavior might also be used as justification for why the whimperer should get what he or she wants. All the emotional pain associated with wanting something or the feeling of trauma that results from not getting it is regarded as justification in itself: The overwhelming pain makes the individual "deserving" of the thing she or he wants. Again, the target person, although supposed to respond positively to the whimpering might get turned off by it and leave the scene without complying with the needs of the whimperer.

Is there a better way of getting what we want? The philosophy and operating system that persons in pain use may seem to indicate that pain makes us deserving of or entitled to getting what we want, that is, seeing pain or disappointment as entitlement. Physical illnesses and emotional disturbances can serve controlling functions, even when the afflicted person is not fully aware of the underlying dynamics. Most people would be only too willing to help a friend or family member who is in distress. Comfort and assistance are dispensed freely and easily in the beginning. As time goes on, however, what once was cheerfully given comes to feel like an extra burden that is expected by the suffering person; previously voluntary offerings begin to feel like obligations or sacrifices. Just as the sufferer gets comfortable in the receiving position, the helper begins to withdraw. Stronger emphasis of their needs may assist sufferers in temporarily continuing their control. In the end, the good Samaritans will find ways to distance themselves geographically or emotionally from the sufferer.

Exaggerated or unrealistic demands as attempts to control others may backfire even faster, especially when they are presented as threats. Unless for some reason the threatened person is completely dependent on the controller, removal is the first strategy that will come to the mind of the threatened target person. The speed of removal is usually inversely related to the degree of dependency the target person feels toward the controlling person. The more dependent the person perceives himself or herself to be, the slower will be the removal.

Most likely, there are just as many control techniques that backfire, as there are methods that can be worked successfully. And mastering self-control includes as many opportunities for failure as does mastering control over others. Throughout the book there will be opportunities to study both.

4 ▪ ▪ ▪

Contestants in the Control Dance

When talking about control techniques, we instantly focus on efforts directed at us by people in our immediate environment: people we know and may have observed for some time. Those who have influenced our actions at times, though we might not have been aware of it until later, come to mind readily. The emotional impact from having been taken advantage of by those we know is much stronger than when we think about control in abstract terms. When institutions exercise control over our lives, although often equally detrimental to our interests, it seems more remote. We accept a certain degree of helplessness more easily in those situations.

Perhaps the difference in our emotional reactions is due to the difference in the scale of the control attempts. When we become aware of it in interactions with those we know, we may think that we should have been able to prevent being taken advantage of. A significant portion of our emotional response, most likely anger, is directed at ourselves. The situation assumes the flavor of a personal competition, whereas when control operates on a larger scale, we, like many others, may resign ourselves to being defenseless in the face of the larger power.

▓ Control Tactics from Those We Know

Thomas felt relieved when Andrew suggested they attend the Rotary Club's dinner meeting together. This month's meeting was to be held in an area of town unfamiliar to Thomas. With his poor night vision Thomas, thinking that Andrew would drive, agreed readily. On the morning of the meeting day Thomas received a call from Andrew, informing him that Andrew's car was in the repair shop but would be ready by the time they would go to the meeting. Would Thomas mind driving Andrew to the shop, which is nearby and they could proceed from there, parking Thomas's car at the shop? Andrew's request seemed harmless enough and Thomas agreed.

When Thomas arrived at Andrew's office to drive him to the repair shop, Andrew apologized; the repair shop just called to let him know that the car was not ready. They would have to drive Thomas's car to the meeting. Thomas felt anxious about driving to and from the meeting, as it was getting dark already. Worrying about the drive home, Thomas could not concentrate on the content of the meeting. Finally it was time to leave. Andrew suddenly remembered that he had agreed to pick up his wife Sally from her evening exercise class. It was not much of a detour, he reassured Thomas. Driving slowly, Thomas managed to find the location of Sally's class.

Sally was irritable; she had been waiting for some time. Andrew apologized and explained that his car was still in the repair shop. "How are you going to get to work tomorrow morning," inquired Sally. "Don't you remember that your son drove my car back to college?" A classmate had dropped him off because of trouble with his own old car. As an explanation addressed to Thomas she added, "Our son was planning on driving my car back when he comes home in a couple of weeks"

Although Sally's question was directed at Andrew, Thomas felt it as a confrontation to him, and he quickly offered to pick up Andrew on his way to work the next morning. Although he realized that this might not be the end of the story, because there was still Andrew's car that needed to be picked up from the repair shop when ready. By now Thomas was so anxious about still having to drive home in the dark that he decided not to waste any more time coming up with solutions about Andrew's transportation to work. Thomas made it home safely, but he was stressed out from the tension. Later he remembered a similar situation involving Andrew that had occurred less than a year ago. Was this coincidence, or was it Andrew's way of ensuring that he had a convenient ride while his car was being repaired?

People in situations similar to that of Thomas may complain: "I did not realize that my colleague (or my neighbor, or my friend) tried to control me. By the time I became aware of it, it was too late." Although it is sad and unfortunate to discover someone's control attempts late in the game, it is never too late to learn from them. With the experience of controlling behaviors the questions arise who exerts the control and to what purpose? Sometimes the control techniques employed appear obvious; at other times they remain hidden for a while.

Control-related behaviors have one thing in common with other behaviors—they are purposeful. They have goals and they have targets. They also have outcomes. Like other purposeful behaviors—if they are successful, the person using them will most likely use them again. Successful actions will be repeated for the achievement of future successes. For that reason, it is never too late for the victim to discover the workings of control attempts. As in the case of Thomas and Andrew above, Thomas remembered a similar experience in the past; however, his attention was not sufficiently focused at the time, and it took a second occasion for him to learn the lesson.

■ Controlling Friends

In order to feel safe and valued, individuals form emotional bonds to friends and family. We trust them and disclose to them our dreams, fears, and wishes, hoping that they will not disappoint us. Conversely, those who are not true friends can use the knowledge of our disclosures to manipulate us. "A person who knows how to appeal to our emotions can deceive us, manipulate us, and get us to accept as true that which is untrue" (Gula, 2002, p. 4). Knowing how we respond to certain emotional strikes can be used in triggering a particular emotion that will direct our actions away from our objective. In other words, knowing a person's "anger buttons" can be helpful in distracting the person from pursuing his or her goals successfully, as explained in an earlier chapter.

Interactions between close friends, in addition to the exchange of warm feelings, provide occasions for application of control tactics because the people involved have so many opportunities to study the emotional makeup and the behavior of those with whom they interact frequently. It is not difficult to predict individuals' actions, having previously observed the connection between their feelings and actions. Triggering a person's emotional reactions may set off a string of behaviors that are advantageous to the controller but detrimental to the person thus controlled. In this scenario the emotionally entangled individual loses the advantage that comes from planned actions while attempting to cope with the surprising actions originating from the controller.

Tina and Betty had been close friends for many years. They planned and enjoyed many activities together. Betty, the older of the two, was quick to anger in addition to being sensitive about being rejected. Tina, acknowledging many good qualities in her friend, had learned to use Betty's anger to navigate around the rejection issue. Tina knew that if Betty felt rejected by Tina, she would never forgive her. Although the two friends enjoyed each other's company, at times Tina preferred to explore things on her own but she did not dare tell Betty about it. However, keeping it a secret was not a valid option for protecting Betty from feeling rejected once she found out about it later.

Desperate, Tina thought of a solution: if she managed to make Betty angry just before a planned outing, Betty would respond by not accompanying Tina. Betty would be angry, but Tina got her wish of being by herself without risking termination of the friendship. Although Betty's anger was unpleasant to deal with for the moment, with the proper apology from Tina it would pass with time. The prospect of losing her friend's good will forever was, for reasons of her own, more traumatic in Tina's mind than the temporary discomfort of being subjected to Betty's anger.

Of course, one could argue whether it was actually in Tina's best interest to induce her friend's anger in order to occasionally achieve her preferences. If Betty ever caught on to Tina's manipulations, that would surely be the end of the friendship. Perhaps a better approach would be to openly and honestly discuss the situation with Betty and place the responsibility for the conditions of their friendship, at least in part, on Betty. However, one should not underestimate the power of reinforcement that works in situations like this. After Tina had enjoyed her solo trips and her apology was rewarded with forgiveness, naturally Tina felt immense relief. That relief reinforced the notion that she had just managed to navigate through a difficult situation and that she had done the correct thing—everything was well again.

As neutral observers we can often think of various alternatives that seem to be unavailable to those deeply involved in the situation. What accounts for the individual's focus on one path as solution to a problem and failure to consider alternatives? Actions and emotions are based in underlying beliefs and attitudes. People behave in accordance with their undisputed beliefs. In addition, as long as their actions have not seriously harmed them (to the point of death?), people believe that their schemes have worked for them, and therefore they will be easily persuaded to apply them again when needed. After all, why discard something that seems to work?

If Tina had believed in the existence of a viable alternative, she would most likely have made use of it. Depending on the frequency of its occurrence, one wonders how long it will take for Betty to recognize Tina's manipulations. Tina was not proud of the fact that she manipulated her friend's feelings, but she tried to reassure herself that she was doing this to protect her friend from even worse negative emotions, those that come from feeling rejected. Again, as mentioned above, the feeling of relief confirmed in Tina's mind that her actions were correct. In reality, Tina's justification also served to protect her self-image to herself.

People are convinced that holding on to beliefs and convictions are part of one's character. Otherwise we would just act whimsically in unpredictable ways, whichever way the wind blows. Of course, our beliefs and values give meaning to what we do, and the conviction that we are doing the "right" thing often lends strength to our actions—even in cases where the actions are not in our best interest. Thus, much like the effect of one's expectations discussed in Chapter 1, firmly held beliefs control our decisions and actions, for good or bad.

▒ Beliefs and Their Role in Control Situations

Listening empathically to others who have suffered the pain of loss or disappointments and attempting to reduce their discomfort and motivate them to go on with their life would concur with most people's beliefs. When others begin disclosing their emotions, we often unwittingly encourage them to do so, and we express varying degrees of sympathy or empathy with the person who seems consumed with sad emotions. We may feel sorry for them and become more involved than we originally wanted to.

Louise, a young widow with two daughters tried to console a male co-worker who appeared devastated because his fiancée broke off their engagement. Having found a willing sympathetic ear, the coworker paid daily visits to Louise's home to unload his emotional pain. The presence of her daughters did not seem to deter him. Louise felt sorry for him but also was uncomfortable about the way he had invaded her life. She continued to tolerate his daily visits for a bit longer—to help him over the toughest time, she told herself. Just as she was about to tell him not to stop by at her home anymore, he attempted to attack her sexually. As she told him in no uncertain terms to leave, she thought that this would be the end of the involvement.

However, she was mistaken; he stalked her, appearing in front of her house and at the supermarket nearby. He tried to talk to her neighbors and spread nasty rumors about her at work. In telephone calls to her home he accused her of having led him on, only to reject him, and of having taken advantage of him when he was vulnerable. He also threatened to get even with her. Louise feared for her daughters' safety as well as for her own. She considered the possibility of a restraining order but was discouraged by horror stories involving people who had sought this solution. Several months later she found a job in a different town and quietly moved away with her daughters.

Looking more closely at Louise's situation reveals that the moment when she felt uncomfortable about the coworker's habitual visits to her home, she received the signal that he had placed himself in a position of control. Feeling sorry for him overshadowed her awareness of the signal and kept her from recognizing her own growing vulnerability in the situation. Her hesitation in acting on the forewarning became costly.

Joan, a young professional married to an attorney who had the habit of intimidating her with his questions, joined a growth group to improve her communication skills. "If I don't have the answers to one question, he asks another question. But when *I* ask questions he gets mad," she told the group. Asked how she interpreted her husband's behavior for herself, she responded, "If he doesn't like it, he should understand that I don't like it either!" With some prompting, the group leader led Joan to express her underlying belief in the situation: "You should not do to others what you don't want to have happen to you—isn't that the Golden Rule—to treat others as you would want to be treated?" The group leader emphasized that this was Joan's belief, but was it also her husband's belief? Joan was stunned; she thought it was everybody's belief.

This verbal interchange demonstrated how deeply entrenched and how influential some of our beliefs are and how little we are aware of the full extent of their impact on our behavior and our expectations of the behaviors of others. In general, we act as if our beliefs are true for us and for other people too. By assuming that our beliefs are universal and held by everybody else, we render ourselves vulnerable to control actions from others.

▨ Control in Intimate Relationships

Intimate relationships provide a wide range of territory for the application of control approaches. In some relationships a one-sided power situation can be observed early on, perhaps due to the selection criteria of the involved partners; in other unions it may develop over time. Julia, a beautiful brunette in her late 30s, had always been attracted to intelligent men, possibly for the wrong reasons because her relationships had not been happy ones for her. In her first marriage, which she entered shortly after graduating from college, she became disillusioned after less than three years. Soon after the divorce she met Kirk, her current husband. Kirk graduated at the top of his class and held advanced science degrees. He enjoyed early promotions in the company he worked for, but lately there had been some tension between Kirk and his coworkers. Apparently, some of his colleagues tended to disagree with Kirk's decisions on the job.

What disturbed the harmony at home was, according to Julia, that Kirk was always right. Even when evidence to the contrary stared him in the face, he turned it around, insisting that he was correct after all. He told Julia and their three children what to do and what friends to have. He had a tendency to lecture them at length, usually ending with an irrefutable statement that forced them to agree, even if they disagreed with the content of his arguments.

Julia's response to Kirk's lectures had been withdrawal. After years of arguing and trying to assert her opinions, she had given up and stopped listening. Only occasionally did she flare up about an issue that was important to her. Yet the price was too high because Kirk would push relentlessly until she gave in and let him have his way. Because Kirk was convinced of the correctness of his opinions, he had made some decisions that threatened the family's financial stability. Despite Kirk's good salary, the family's future appeared anything but secure. Furthermore, probably because of the stress he was experiencing, Kirk's lectures and tirades had increased in frequency and intensity.

Julia realized that the time for acquiescence was over. She blamed herself for taking the easy way out and not having been more assertive about Kirk's financial decisions. Could she have stopped him in some of his decisions? She did not believe so. What were her options at this point? Julia's attention was caught by an advertisement about an ongoing workshop like the one mentioned in the introduction to this book for people dealing with control issues. She decided to join the workshop; her experiences will be reported in later chapters of this book.

Other paths of control in intimate relationships were explored with students in a college psychology class, who volunteered personal information about control issues in their own lives. There were those who freely admitted to their own control schemes in various settings. Those who saw themselves as being controlled by others were mainly females. Interestingly, not one of the male students reported that he had been at the receiving end of control attempts by others. Two of them, however, described how they had manipulated their girl friends into doing library research for them or typing their term papers and faxing them to their professors. Considering the fact that control is prevalent in all aspects of life, one wonders whether the male students had not been aware of any control attempt directed at them or whether they did not want to admit that it had happened to them, too.

Several of the young women who saw themselves as victims of control behaviors actually ended up marrying a controlling man, and one of them is still married to him. After more than 15 years of marriage Nancy said, "I have never been out with my friends anywhere. Not to dinner, or a movie, or even just to meet at the mall for a day of shopping. The sad thing is that I now don't even ask, because it will just bring about an argument that will continue for hours and often days." Nancy's husband does not indulge in physical violence anymore, but he still controls her activities—although he does allow her to work outside the home. She craves freedom and she daydreams of a time when she will be independent. Perhaps she is waiting for her children to grow up before she makes a move. From her report, one does not get the impression of any active planning for escape; her fear of the consequences keeps her paralyzed.

Nancy had prior warnings. During the early stage of their relationship she endured physical and emotional abuse, which at times would persuade her to move back into her parents' home, only to return to her husband because she craved his attention. Even now as she daydreams about freedom, and as she says, is weighing her options, she is convincing herself that her husband has deep loving feelings for her. Yet in spite of his love, his questioning and manipulative behaviors have not stopped. As Gavin deBecker (1997) would say, Nancy is beyond being a victim; she has become a volunteer in her own victimization.

Helen, too, had early warnings. A helpful state trooper rescued her and her sister on the highway when her car broke down. He lost no time in finding out where she lived and persuaded her sister to help set up a date. He seemed so protective and was so attentive. Within a month, they were talking about marriage, even though Helen thought it would be advisable to wait for a year before getting married. Nevertheless, he succeeded in manipulating her into marrying him four months after they had met. Soon after the wedding, his seemingly protective behavior gave way to domineering and controlling actions. Helen hardly saw her friends anymore. Her new husband also pushed her into asking her parents for a loan to buy a house. Helen's own savings were soon depleted, and when she finally left the marriage, she lost everything she ever had.

Helen considered herself lucky that her marriage remained childless. The warning signs that she recognized in retrospect included her husband's disregard for her wishes and pursuit of his goal—which was perhaps to obtain her family's money—by speeding up their wedding date. Other signs for concern were a previous marriage he did not talk much about and his disrespectful behavior toward his mother and sister, which might have been predictive of his treatment of Helen. Like many others, Helen did not expect to be manipulated by her future spouse and therefore neglected to take those signs seriously. Part of the reason why control works so well is that often the targets themselves explain away their position as target by justifying it with something else, such as being loved and desired by the controller whose presumable goal it is to make them happy. Why else would they want to marry them?

As Helen—and other women—experienced the transition from the husband's protective to more or less subtly controlling and domineering behavior, intimidation plays an increasingly greater part in the couple's interactions. A female district court judge described her experiences when presiding over domestic abuse cases. Often the participants' body language expresses the underlying dynamics more eloquently than words could do. Women usually present themselves with downcast eyes, stooped shoulders, and monotone, barely audible voices, even though there are now effective support systems in place for the female victims of domestic abuse. The men more often display a defiant attitude, radiating power by casting intimidating glances at their environment, including the female judges, and culminating in a threatening stance toward their female victims.

The district court judge described a recent case in which the husband had violated the restraining order previously issued by the court; the wife had filed a complaint about his ongoing harassment of her. Soon after her husband entered the courtroom, the wife's behavior turned from reflecting reasonable tension and anxiety to open fear. Before taking his assigned seat, the husband stood erect and turned for a moment toward his wife with his hands held in midair. When the judge observed that the wife stifled a cry and started to shake, she looked closer at the husband's hands—he was holding a dog collar. The judge recognized that this brief scene was the key to the whole case and requested the husband's attorney to bring up the dog collar for her to inspect.

Turning to the wife, she asked her if she could identify the tag on the dog collar. In a quivering voice the wife reported that it was from the family's dog. The collar and tag had disappeared a few days ago. The children had noticed its absence and were worried about it because it was their dog, which they had raised from a puppy. To her children, the dog was just like a member of the family. In the safety of the judge's chamber, the wife was asked for her interpretation of the dog collar's presence in her husband's hands. Shaking and stammering, the wife explained that her husband had wanted to threaten her to withdraw her complaint about his harassment. The children were devoted to the dog and would be heartbroken if anything happened to it. To her, her husband's gesture indicated the threat that the dog would disappear or be killed.

Would the woman have spoken out about her fears while still in the courtroom? Probably not; that's why the judge—after observing the silent interaction between husband and wife—decided on her action. Intimidation is still a powerful tool in the hands of male partners within the confines of the domestic sphere.

The supply of young females willing to be trapped by a controlling lover seems to be never ending, as the mother of Sara, a 14-year-old girl, writing for help to Annie's Mail Box would indicate (Mitchell & Sugar, 2009c). Sara is involved in a relationship with a controlling boyfriend, two years her senior. According to the mother, Sara has changed drastically within the past six months. As result of her boyfriend's insistence, she has withdrawn from her friends and spends the time that she is not with him alone in her room. Sara has admitted to having sex with her boyfriend.

Although the mother had invited the boyfriend to her home, he refused to visit. Instead Sara is begging her mother to drive her over to the boyfriend's home. This 16-year-old boy apparently has stepped up his control techniques and intended targets to include the girl's mother. In his written communication with Sara's mother, the boyfriend has accused her of being a horrible mother and not loving Sara as much as he does. The boy's hold over Sara seems to be increasing in strength; the more the mother tries to keep her daughter away from him, the more she clings to him. His method of control is not restricted to Sara; he unhesitatingly uses intimidation on the girl's mother, too.

From this report, the young girl seems to be heading toward Nancy and Helen's fate described above. As with those two women, there are plenty of warning signs, indicating the degree of controlling behaviors applied by the boyfriend. The social isolation of the victim is just the first step in the classic pattern of the possessive controller. Mental abuse and/or physical abuse are likely to follow. Disregarding the warning signs now will cost Sara a lot more as she chooses to remain connected to him. Now she still has a mother willing to help her get out of this suffocating relationship; later it might be much more difficult to escape.

In connection with the word control, some people may think back to instances of bullying they experienced during their childhood years; a new version of this practice, cyber-bullying, has made its appearance in the life of today's teenagers. Apparently 20 to 30 percent of teens participate in "sexting"—sending nude photos as electronic messages through cell phones, while actually almost 60 percent of teenagers admitted to receiving such suggestive electronic messages (Merritt, 2010). The pressure for sending nude pictures of themselves seems to center mostly on young girls. The story of Jesse Logan, a high school student from Ohio who sent a nude picture of herself to her boyfriend, describes the tragic consequences of this practice. After Jesse and her boyfriend ended their relationship, the boyfriend sent Jesse's picture to the entire high school. Ridiculed, harassed, and taunted for months, Jesse finally committed suicide. While prosecutors and the Juvenile Department of Correction debate whether sexting constitutes a C or D level felony, who is there to advise young girls like Jesse on how not to become a victim of this type of pressure?

Most reports of control scenarios in the personal sphere of life come from individuals who are convinced that they have been victims. Melanie was the exception. She admitted to having manipulated every romantic relationship she had ever been involved in—with negative results. Although she considered herself a good and caring person, she had been aware of her control attempts for a long time. Whoever the significant man in her life was at the time, Melanie wanted to control his activities and insisted on his being with her at all times. What did she offer in return? Sex combined with the threat of ending the relationship (stop the sex) if he did not comply with her terms. However, in her fear of being abandoned, she tried to find out what the men wanted in a perfect woman and then she worked hard to supply it. None of her relationships lasted, even her 15-year marriage finally failed mostly because of her controlling ways.

After repeated failures, why did Melanie continue with her manipula-tions? Melanie knew the reasons for her self-defeating behaviors: insecur-ity and fear of abandonment. For many years, she combated those fears with sex, money, and threats of leaving—always with the result of being left. Had awareness of the reasons for her manipulative behaviors helped her to learn a lesson? Not yet: at the most recent contact with her, she was dating several men with different characteristics, different professions, and different goals for a relationship. With each one of them, Melanie tried to be exactly the woman he is looking for—except for her controlling tactics. However, she was mentally exhausted from playing different roles, employing many of the same techniques. Melanie may not know how to change her behaviors, but she was also afraid of giving up those behaviors. Because the men stayed with her for varying periods of time, she told her-self that her approach was working—at least, better than anything else she could think of. Her reasoning is not unique; as described earlier, most peo-ple maintain behaviors that overall are self-defeating but successful part of the time because they don't know what the alternatives would bring.

Ideally, in romantic relationships and marriages we don't want to con-sider control issues, partly perhaps because of the belief that intimate rela-tionships are based on love, not control, and if we don't expect it, we don't look for it. In addition, the exercise of control in intimate relation-ships is subtle because it may not be displayed on a daily basis (Strong, DeVault, & Cohen, 2005). In another plea to Annie's Mailbox (Mitchell & Sugar 2009d), a woman reported having raised her stepdaughter for the past 10 years. Although having treated her well and supported her for all these years, the stepdaughter wanted to leave the home and move in with a friend. Knowing that her father would be on her side, the girl told him her decision to move out was because of the stepmother. According to the reader requesting advice, her marriage almost broke up because of this situation.

Should she talk to her stepdaughter and explain how hurt she has been was the reader's question to Annie. Annie did not think that was a good idea, but what does the reader's plea say about her relationship to her hus-band? If he were willing to let his daughter control his life and his rela-tionship to his wife, how devoted was he to his wife? Annie did not respond to this aspect of the situation.

■ Emotional State and Physically Violent Control

The display of strong negative emotions, such as anger, can be and often is meant to serve a control function. The person displaying the anger wants to threaten that noncompliance with the person's wishes will result in harsh punishment for the offending person. Often such intimidation works, at least, for a while. Sometimes it is a small step from intimidation to physical violence. In the domestic violence literature violent men are described as preoccupied with control issues. These men interpret masculinity as having control over themselves, their intimate partners, their children, and their environments (Anderson & Umberson, 2001). The male as the absolute "king of his castle" is still a masculine ideal.

At the extreme end of marital conflict, domestic violence cases can be regarded as a battle for dominance involving physical, psychological, and sexual abuse as modalities of asserting control. Because all three types of abuse behaviors constitute attempts at control, the discussion of various personality patterns in connection with related underlying variables is relevant to the content of this book. Knowledge about the attachment styles that some of the abusive men have adopted in the past, may warn an intended victim or target of behavior patterns that can be expected.

In general, individuals' attachment styles become more readily observable in stressful situations. So-called instrumental abusers appear to have a high preoccupation with their spouses, a strong spouse-specific dependency. These are the ones who need to know where their spouses are at any moment and what they are doing. They strongly resent any attention their spouses may direct at others or at activities not directly related to the abuser.

A study, involving 79 physically abusive men and a control sample of 44 working-class men, demonstrated that although both types of abusive men (impulsive and instrumental) reported a preoccupied attachment style; the combination of preoccupied with fearful attachment style, was reported only by impulsive men (Tweed & Dutton, 1998). The instrumental-preoccupied combination most likely will result in a consistent, planned application of controlling or abusive behaviors, not reflective of a fearful attachment condition.

Control of the spouse is thought to be the main element in battering, as the violent men believe that any method for establishing control is justified (Jacobson & Gottman, 1998), but others point out that in the framework of intimate terrorism control is established not only through physical violence but also through economic subordination, threats, isolation, and other factors (Johnson, 1995). Systematic use of violence as well as nonviolent coercive control are meant to subordinate, isolate, and increase the woman's emotional and financial dependence on the male partner (Hamby & Sugarman, 1999).

Although not specifically spelled out in all cases, a sense of insecurity in the controlling person seems to be implied in many of the controllers' behaviors. This may not be of primary importance for the target person, but it would present an interesting piece of information in the overall consideration of control schemes. Insecurity can be assumed as a factor in the troubled relationships of income- or status-reversal situations between the two partners. Generally, in Western society, it is expected that higher status and higher income are associated with male rather than female social situations. Therefore, a male partner who is of lower social status or earns a lower income than his female partner is likely to experience feelings of insecurity. To compensate for this reversal in status or income, the man may engage in controlling or coercive behaviors.

Therefore, findings that as a woman's educational attainment significantly increases above that of her husband, the likelihood of emotional abuse directed at her also increases are not surprising (Kaukinen, 2004). Lower educational attainment can translate into lower income and as men's economic resources might be more limited than those of their female partners, the tendency to reassert their control through a variety of emotional abuse tactics grows.

Because physical violence is a severe form of control, it has been given attention here. Unfortunately, the findings from the various research studies that focused on physical violence are inconclusive and perhaps even contradictory in nature. What advice can we offer the recipients or targets of this rather drastic form of control? Suggestions to leave a spouse in times of slim financial resources because of possible physical violence might not be appropriate. Another advice seeker in the column Annie's Mailbox described the following case of a young female coworker who appeared at the office with a horrible black eye. Her boyfriend had punched her in the face in front of her children and friends. While the advice seeker spent the day performing her coworker's job, the victim spent the day worrying about her own and her children's safety as she read the boyfriend's abusive and threatening text messages (Mitchell & Sugar 2009e).

Although the young woman promised never to see the abusive boyfriend again, they got back together, and the advice seeker wondered how to structure her contact with the victim within their working relationship. Offering advice to the victim did not seem to be a workable approach.

Most of the research focusing on external factors for reasons of intimate violence has done little to ease the pain and frustration of those involved in it. Possible external causes that have been indicated in the investigations don't lend themselves to being foundations for practical solutions of the problem. Reframing the issue of domestic violence in simple terms of control dynamics allows for constructive exploration through observation of an individual's overt behavior in combination with assumed underlying cognitive processes that produce a warning sign. For instance, insistence on determining a partner's actions at all times can be understood as a precursor to violence when the insistence does not bring the desired results.

▓ Lady Macbeth, Cleopatra, and the Modern Women

Not all control attempts in intimate relationships are associated with physical aggression. In fact, most control situations involve invisible bruises: the internal damage and pain associated with being the target of control or power struggles, and men are not the only inhabitants of the controller's domain. Striving for control is not a gender-specific phenomenon. Women have their place in the overall scheme.

Shakespeare's Lady Macbeth has become the archetype of the scheming, manipulating woman. She does it all for her husband, to see him become king, and she succeeds, but in the end she kills herself. Then there is Cleopatra, or rather the myth of her. Apparently, in reality she was a plain woman and a capable administrator, but has been described by Octavius Caesar's historians as a temptress who seduced Antony (Whitney & Packer, 2000). According to that version of history, Cleopatra exerted her sexual powers to get what she wanted. Finally, when she was not assured of victory over Octavius Caesar on her terms, she decided to kill herself.

Less dramatic and less publicized are the activities of many of the women living in our times. Barbara, a smart woman liked to go shopping and visiting in the afternoons. Her husband preferred for her to stay closer to the house. Rather than upset or argue with her husband she devised a clever scheme. On the afternoons that she wanted to go out, she set the dinner table early in the day and prepared parts of the meal. She had bits of bacon cut up and some onions nicely stored in the refrigerator. The tea-kettle was filled with water, and off she went. She returned to the home shortly before her husband's arrival from work, just barely in time to turn on the stove, dump the bacon and onions in the frying pan to make the house smell as if she had cooked all afternoon. Barbara made it a point to greet her husband at the door—actually she was not very far from it anyway, hanging up her coat from the afternoon outing.

Barbara then encouraged her husband to relax with a cup of coffee at the table while she applied the—what she called—"finishing touches" to the meal. To stretch the time she invited him to entertain her with work stories, often serving him another cup of coffee. Of course, for the scheme to work, Barbara had to apply the coffee routine every day—whether she went out in the afternoon or not. When the husband met with business associates or friends at a restaurant for a meal, he always made sure to have coffee served before the food arrived. Once he was asked by his dinner companions why he started the meal with coffee instead of having tea or coffee at the end of the meal like most people. His answer was that he had always done it this way. After more than 30 years of marriage, he did not know why he was drinking coffee before eating his meals, but it did not seem to bother him.

Probably many married women have resorted to control schemes like Barbara's, often because they thought they had to, due to their financial dependence on their husbands. However, married women are not the only females employing control strategies or manipulation tactics. If one is to believe the media and popular literature—giving advice on TV and radio programs and in newspapers, magazines, and self-help books, young women are encouraged to apply cleverly worked out routines and behavioral directions in order to attract and capture potential husbands. The reader is referred for additional information to Jaclyn Geller's (2001) thorough report of these practices in her book *Here Comes the Bride*.

▓ It Takes Two to Tango

To comprehend the dynamics in a controller-controllee relationship to its full extent, it is necessary to understand the personality patterns of all the people involved, not just that of the controlling person. Although the controlling person may manipulate or victimize the target person, in most cases this cannot happen without the active participation of the controlled person in the relationship. What brings the controller and the controllee together and what keeps them together? The two seem to attract each other like magnets. At first, the controlled person might admire a sense of decisiveness, determination, or strength in the other, especially if it is a romantic relationship between female controllee and male controller. Although an element of control can be detected early in the relationship, the controllee is often inclined to explain it away with statements like, "He is so concerned for my well-being; it is really an expression of his love for me" when he insists on knowing where she is at every moment.

A controlling relationship evolves over time. The participants gradually develop a kinship because of something inside themselves that they have in common. As they disclose events from their past, they also disclose past painful occurrences. One of the two participants may decide to use the other's painful experience as a vehicle for control. When that occurs, the other person had better recognize and remember the familiar behavioral signs of the controller and the familiar pain. Now is the time to exit.

Some believe that in controlling relationships both parties experience self-doubt and poor self-esteem and that both sides are trying to protect themselves from the hurt of rejection (Stenack, 2001, p. 41): "There is no reason for aggression between people other than fear. Controllers are people with fear. The fear is related to their own underlying self-doubt and sense of inadequacy. They use this self-doubt and insecurity as a weapon to gain control over others. . . . Controllers are not operating from strength but from fear." Although this is a valid point, the person who becomes the target of controlling behaviors would be well advised to focus more on the controlling strategies than on the reasons why the controller is engaging in this behavior. As the recipient of victimizing behavior, it is not the time or place to develop feelings of empathy with or sympathy for the controller. A word of advice to target persons: Understanding the controller's reason is less important than the target's well-being.

Stenack's warning that the controller has less invested in the words used than in the act of controlling makes an important point. The controller's words are meant to draw the victim into an interaction in which the controlling behavior can be applied. Therefore, it is important to be aware of the difference between content and process. Content is what is actually being said between people. When focusing on content alone, individuals become stuck in the verbal conversation. That is, they can only deal with the things that are actually being said, but there is an entirely different way of participating in a conversation. One can focus on the process, rather than the content. In other words, the person selected as the to-be-controlled target would do well observing the process rather than becoming a forced participant discussing the content.

▓ The Approach—Avoidance Dance

To remain in the observer position is good advice for those who become involved with a person being afraid of engulfment and avoiding commitments. In romantic relationships, this is most commonly the male partner. Often at the beginning of a relationship, the commitment avoider appears quite invested in the development of the relationship; he may even utter such vague verbal promises as, "You are the person I'd like to grow old with," or "If we were to have children, I would like the girls to look like you," or "Next year around this time would seem nice for an engagement." These statements have the sound of commitments, but the commitments are conditional and the conditions are never defined. Unfortunately, the hopeful female partner in this dance of approach–avoidance usually limits her hearing to the words that seem to express commitment. With that she firmly enters the commitment path, which becomes more and more controlled by her partner.

With her first few steps on the commitment path her partner begins to withdraw. Although his words may not be very different for a while, the process, his behavior, is changing in subtle ways. He may not be as freely available as in the past; his friends or family members may suddenly need his help, or he may have to work overtime. There is a positive correlation between the degree of subtleness and the time period he can allow for the process of retreating. His changing behaviors might elicit a slight feeling of confusion in her, but she is still listening to the sounds of his words. As her confusion increases, she might even attempt to discuss her feelings with him. This is the moment for him to reassure her that his feelings for her are true, but he may also caution her about the risks of making hasty decisions. The more she tries to convince him that there are no risks because they both know what they want, the more he cautions—and withdraws.

To the uninvolved observer it becomes obvious that the male partner in this scenario has been in control of the development of the relationship, both in terms of speed and direction. The emotionally involved participant who focused mainly on the words uttered previously, even when the actions were no longer congruent with the words, is left dangling in a vacuum that she has difficulty comprehending.

▓ Control as Relationship Glue

Other scenarios reflect a dance of control, with both partners knowingly participating, although complaining and blaming the other. The dynamics in these interactive control situations are such that one wonders what would happen to the relationship if the reasons for the controlling behaviors were eliminated. Without that element, it seems that the relationship would simply disintegrate. This is the type of control framework in which some couples, such as controlling wives and their resentful husbands who have been accused or convicted of having committed various sexual offenses, operate.

A small group of men referred by their lawyers or by the court system represented such a dance of control in their private lives. Four of the men had been convicted of exposing themselves in public. For two of them, Joshua and Norman, it was the first time that they had been caught; the other two had anywhere from two to four prior convictions. All four complained about the unfairness of the judicial system: after all, they had not hurt anyone. Joshua, the youngest of the four had been picked up in the parking lot of a shopping mall. He insisted that he had no intention of exposing himself. He had needed to use a toilet. Why did he not go into one of the several stores with public restrooms in the mall? His answer was that he did not know where the restrooms were and that he could not wait much longer, so he had decided to relieve himself into a bottle while he was in his car. The judge did not believe the story, but it was his first known offense, and the judge put him on probation with the condition of participation in counseling.

Norman, a married man with four children was uncertain about his gender identity. Lately, his urges to try out homosexual relationships had become stronger, and he acted on those urges by exposing himself in a public place where he expected that men with similar desires would approach him. Instead, he made the acquaintance of an undercover police officer. Bruce had been caught twice over a period of six years, and Harry, the oldest of the three, had been picked up four times during the past 20 years. All four men were married, although Joshua and his wife had only been married for about six months. Bruce and Harry had two children each.

The wives of the four men were interviewed separately. Joshua's wife believed her husband's story and blamed the legal system for persecuting

Joshua. Norman's wife appeared distraught. She briefly considered divorce rather than helping Norman and his attorney to keep the situation quiet. The temptation to get back at her parents-in-law, who had disapproved of Norman's marriage to her, was great; however, she did not know how to cope on her own with four children. She certainly could not expect any assistance from Norman's parents if she made the reason for divorce public.

The wives of Bruce and Harry seemed emotionally aloof. They did not defend their husbands because they knew that the charges against them were true. Both accepted the situation but left no doubt that they had no interest in participating in any of the counseling. They felt that they were punished already with the embarrassment over their husbands' activities. They showed thinly veiled disgust, but when asked what made them stay with their husbands, they both agreed that it was for the sake of their children. According to their reports, their sex life was sporadic at best, but when questioned in more detail, the wives admitted that they had no interest in engaging in sexual activities with their husbands. Both blamed their husbands' deviant behaviors for their lack of sexual interest.

Meanwhile Norman complained about having to do most of the household chores and taking care of the children because his wife was too depressed to function adequately. Both Bruce and Harry complained about their wives' bossiness. Harry was able to escape most of it because he was a truck driver for a major trucking firm. Harry had been able to obtain this employment due to the fact that his most recent conviction was several years ago and his attorney had negotiated a longer than usual probation period in exchange for confidentiality. However, if Harry violated probation, he would lose the consideration of confidentiality and with that his job. He could not imagine a life staying at home with his wife and children.

On the other hand, Bruce, with a good job as a professional, was exposed to everyday home life. He complained bitterly that his wife was sending him out on errands whenever she had forgotten certain items. His wife also worked full time, and she assumed responsibility for getting the children off to school and picking them up from the after-school childcare agency because she could not trust Bruce with that task. Bruce felt that his wife treated him more like a servant than a husband. If he complained to her, she would hint that his parents would not be happy to find out about his legal problems. That was enough for Bruce to do what he had been told. His anger and bitterness increased.

First, he was angry about having been charged with indecent exposure. After all, he had been standing in the window of his own bedroom when he fondled his penis. In the privacy of his own home he should be allowed to do what he wanted, and the woman across the small courtyard of the apartment complex did not have to look at his window. Of course, he admitted later that he had chosen the time to expose himself when he knew that she was at home. He also purposefully "forgot" to close the drapes at his own window. Also, the young woman across the courtyard was not the first to inform the police. The first official complaint came from the parents of one of his children's playmates. The children's friends came over on Saturday mornings to play. One Saturday morning he took a shower when the children were there. He left the bathroom just covered by his bathrobe, and when the children started talking to him, he sat down with them.

After a while three of the children went to another room, leaving just the little neighbor girl. Bruce's bathrobe had no zipper or buttons and was held together only by a belt. With a little bit of movement, the robe opened and exposed his genitals. Bruce was aware of it but acted as if he had not noticed, wondering to himself how the girl would react to it. She said nothing, but she must have told her parents about it. Bruce's wife had not been at home that morning. Saturday mornings were her time for working out at the health club.

As Bruce's anger increased so did his level of stress. He claimed that it was during stressful times that he was most vulnerable to fantasize and act out the scenarios in his mind. His wife with her domineering and controlling behaviors was to blame for the buildup of anxiety and stress. Whenever he attempted to avoid some of the tasks she had lined up for him, she reminded him that she could not even leave him alone with their own children. She had to be with them at all times when they were at home. It was bad enough that she had no time for herself anymore.

Just the week before, she had called the therapist to report that she had observed Bruce undress himself in front of the bedroom window as she walked in. Without a word she closed the drapes and walked out. Her silence spoke loud and clear. Interestingly, Bruce had not mentioned the situation to the therapist.

The therapeutic concerns of these cases are beyond the scope of this book, but it is obvious that the wives of Norman, Harry, and Bruce used their husbands' deviant activities as the basis for controlling them in some ways, especially Norman and Bruce's wives were in a position to dominate them. Although Norman's wife left the children in her husband's care, the other two women built up a life with their children. Neither one was interested in an emotionally or physically intimate relationship with her husband at this time, but they apparently did not mind having them around to help provide for the family and perform chores as they determined. They may not have been completely happy, but life was bearable so long as they had the upper hand.

With the help of his attorney, Norman's situation was not made public. Legal fees and counseling kept him safe. Eventually, he obtained employment in another state where he was able to commute home on weekends, but during the week, he was living by himself and enjoying his freedom.

He promised his wife that soon the whole family would be moved to his new residence, but he did all he could to prolong the time before their reunion. Bruce complained bitterly about his wife's "bossiness" but he was the one who provided the opportunities for his own submission.

What may have started out as ill-advised coping mechanisms to suppress or control anxieties that were at the basis of his exhibitionism pulled the net of outside control by his wife around him increasingly tighter. Instead of using the mandated therapy to free himself from his troublesome urges, he resisted exploration of the underlying reasons and thereby increased his vulnerability and his bondage in a marriage that made him feel like a slave. In his mind, his wife's controlling behaviors provided him with the justification for engaging in his sexually acting-out behavior; however, what excuse would he use if he were to be caught again and confronted with imprisonment?

5 ■ ■ ■

Players in the World of Work and Business

Life in the world of work and the larger community requires behaviors that are based in cooperative as well as competitive value systems. Although if one believed some of the advice given in the business literature, cooperative values don't seem to be much in demand. Titles such as *Business Is Combat*, a fighter pilot's guide to winning in modern business warfare (Murphy, 2000), by the president of a company that develops seminars for large businesses, suggests that only competition will make businesses succeed, and competition here has the sound of control in its severest terms. As the author promises: "Business isn't *like* combat; business *is* combat. . . . I am going to turn you into a modern business warrior, a fighter pilot equipped in every way to fight and win the vital battles that are a daily part of your business life. Your transformation from sheep to lion will require a change in your attitude, and that change involves your understanding that business really is combat, in the most visceral and urgent sense" (p. 24).

Murphy's company professes to have some of the finest corporations in the country as clients, and perhaps their successes are largely due to the "warfare" approach, but it is hoped that there is still space for cooperation in the world of business. In fairness to the author, it should be mentioned that he emphasizes the importance of teamwork, which would seem to include cooperation among members of the team, but leaves the field open for combat among different teams. From that point of view, behavioral rules for business settings would condone or even encourage the use of control schemes.

▦ When Business Is Combat, It Pays to Have an Army

Building his own team for combat in the business world was the approach Walter took when developing his system for gaining control and power. When he arrived as the new manager of a country club, he carefully screened all the employees already working for the club. He devoted special attention to those who had some weak points in their background. Ralph, a shy young man whose father had served time for theft, caught his eye. Ralph performed the functions of a handyman, and he could be counted on to handle many tasks. As a social outcast in the small town, Ralph was grateful for his job; he never complained.

Then there was Elaine, a pretty young waitress who seemed as eager to learn as Ralph was eager to work. What was Elaine's weak point? She was the single mother of a son who was conceived out of wedlock. His father left the small town long before the son's birth. With that history, Elaine became another one of the town's social outcasts. The financial responsibility for herself and her son made Elaine willing to work any shift assigned to her.

Walter's continued search into the employees' background discovered Paul, the groundskeeper and chauffeur, who had been fined a few years back for speeding, reckless driving, and leaving the scene of an accident after hitting another car. Furthermore, Paul had not carried collision insurance at the time and was unable to pay for the damages to the other car. The club owner had been a friend of Paul's mother and offered to keep him employed but garnered part of his wages to pay for the repair of the damaged car. Furthermore, he persuaded the owner of the car not to press additional charges against Paul in direct exchange for the money taken out of Paul's paychecks.

Those three, Elaine, Ralph, and Paul seemed the perfect candidates for Walter's plans. Walter took a special interest in them, leading them to trust him and believe that he was on their side. He monitored their work activities closely, encouraging them to take on new responsibilities with vague promises of advancing their positions. Their self-esteem increased gradually, but they never forgot that they were dependent on Walter's good will. In the past, nobody had given them the benefit of the doubt but had judged them according to their vulnerabilities. The three became Walter's stout supporters; they would never let him down. With time their responsibilities grew, and Walter's workload decreased—although not to the outside observer. Walter's goal was simple and straightforward: "More power, less work."

Feeling secure with his three supporters firmly in place, Walter decided to increase his power base by becoming the manager of a larger club in a city located several states away. Knowing that a good part of his power was based in the loyalties of his three special employees, Walter tried hard to persuade them to follow him to the new workplace. He was successful convincing Elaine and Ralph that it would be in their best interest to follow their "benefactor" to the new place. Paul declined to take advantage of this opportunity. As soon as Walter had set up his new territory, he sent for Elaine and Ralph. At this point they had worked for him for about 10 years and believed their future depended on him. Knowing their insecurities, Walter had manipulated and brainwashed them successfully. They saw him as their mentor and protector.

At the new club, Walter made Elaine assistant manager, although her salary did not reflect this; however, Walter reassured her that it would increase with time; she just had to prove herself in the new position. Elaine was easy to persuade; she looked up to Walter—just as she had looked up to her father. She wanted so much to be accepted. Elaine and Ralph worked harder than ever before to allow Walter more time for his managerial oversight and planning. With their hard work they had to set role models for the other employees.

It took Elaine almost another five years to realize Walter's goals. She and the groundskeeper at the new club had taken a liking to each other and got married. Her son was almost 10 years old, and she wanted to take some time to be with him and her new husband for a smooth transition to family life for all three of them, but her workload increased steadily as Walter took off more time for travel and obscure meetings. If she complained, he praised her for her ambition and the progress she had made from the early years as waitress. Thus manipulating her emotions, turning any anger into gratitude with a twinge of guilt mixed in, he continued to control her compliance.

Elaine was not the only one suffering under a heavy workload; Ralph disclosed his disappointment to her and finally some of the other employees complained openly. Walter apparently underestimated the employee's grumbling when he continued his own light work schedule. He had more important things to do with his time. The disgruntled employees found a better listener in the club owner, who—after some investigation—decided not to renew Walter's contract after the five-year period. Walter was stunned but immediately started his job search and informed his wife to give notice at her place of work.

Again, he requested Elaine's promise to join him after he had secured another similar position. Elaine wondered if he expected her to leave her husband; he had not mentioned him at all, but she did not want to uproot her family. Besides she liked her job and the people she worked with. When she refused the promise to join him, Walter accused her of being disloyal. That was when she realized that for more than 15 years Walter had influenced her life according to his goals. She had paid with hard work all those years from the day she had been promoted out of the wait-ress job classification. Her longing for acceptance and approval had made her so vulnerable that she had difficulty setting goals for herself independ-ently of Walter. When she refused to follow him again, she finally was on her way to becoming her own person.

▩ Competitive Values and Control in Business

Is it more acceptable to use and admit controlling behaviors in the work world than in the personal part of our lives? A survey of undergraduate psychology students seemed to indicate that. The students reasoned that in business or work their behaviors do not express anything like a per-sonal attitude toward their targets; it's just a way to make a living. Believ-ing that it was important for them to make as much money as they could, they argued that the end justified the means and that the targets should be able to understand and accept this—in case they were able to figure out the control scheme. Thus, in work situations, the students endorsed a com-petitive value system as the basis for their attitudes.

Many responses came from students who worked part-time in service-related jobs. Doreen, Wanda, and Susan reported their experiences as wait-resses. Their techniques included persuading customers to order more appetizers, desserts, and alcohol than the customers would actually want to purchase. They described, in mouth-watering terms, the different items that they tempted the customers to order or how they pointed out that a customer really gets more for his or her money by ordering a large drink or a whole bottle instead of just settling for a small glass of a beverage. If people hesitated to order a dessert, the waitress tempted them with the suggestion that they could share the dessert because it was really large enough for two—"but it's not fattening!" As the total bill increased, so did their tip and, of course, supplying two plates and cake forks or spoons for one item deserves an extra generous tip.

Then there was the practice of serving the bigger and better cuts of meat to the male customer because in most cases he was the one who paid the bill, which included the decision about the tip. His female companion would not be neglected, however; she might receive a special smile and compliment about her choices from the menu, her wardrobe, jewelry, or whatever could be used to make her feel important.

Wanda added her own successful routines. Of course, she was always friendly, even if a customer behaved in rude or hostile ways. She would not change her approach but maintained full eye contact while smiling at them. To customers of a different ethnic or cultural background she wanted to convey that they would get the best service from her regardless of their background. After a pleasant greeting, she might rest her hand on their shoulder while pointing to a special dish on the menu or answering a question. She would try to pamper them with little "extras" from the kitchen, such as a bite of a different appetizer or side dish. She had no difficulty laughing at customers' corny jokes or comments.

Wanda's activities were not limited strictly to customers; she was always willing to come in early to work and stay late when necessary. She was eager to accommodate another waitress by "subbing" a shift for her. Her accommodating and flexible behaviors assured her the best stations in the restaurant and the highest number of work hours with the largest tips.

Ron, who worked as a server in a popular restaurant, gave special attention to single women. He saw to it that they were seated in a comfortable place, pointing out the advantages of the seating. For instance, he gently pointed out that at this table one was protected from the full blast of the air conditioning or in a few minutes the sun will hit this particular seat at the table, which may be uncomfortable for the female customer. Whatever he could think of to make the single woman feel protected, he would use because more often than not she would reward the "protector" with a generous tip. He had built up a regular female clientele who would flock to his station in the restaurant.

Anne, who had a job in the customer service department of a large department store, was not sure whether or not she manipulated the customers by being nice to them. She remained friendly, and she listened to them when customers complained—even if she thought they were wrong. By giving them the impression that she thought they were right, she defused any confrontation. Anne did not believe her behavior was a bad way to treat customers. She saw it as a workable tool in satisfying the customer. She added, "I am certain they do not feel manipulated, but I think that is probably what I do."

▓ Keeping the Prospective Customer on a Tight Leash

Frank, looking back on his years of working for an automobile dealership, described his experiences. He received special training in selling automobiles from the owner of the business. Every morning started with a practice session where the salesmen used role-playing exercises to hone their sales skills. Advertising costs ran from about $50,000 to $75,000 a month, and their actual sales ratio was about 1 to 5, or 20 percent of the people coming through the doors of the dealership actually bought a car.

According to Frank, customer control received the strongest emphasis during the training. It started with the customary handshake. A salesperson was not supposed to let go of the customer's hand until he knew the customer's name. The second step in the control process was the "follow me" routine. After assessing the customer's needs or wishes, the salesperson led the customer around the car lot. This provides an opportunity to make use of a popular persuasion strategy in sales. By understating the price for the car the customer seems most interested in, the sales person inserts the beginning of what is known as the low-ball technique (Cialdini, 2001). The culmination of this phase is the "invitation" to take a demonstration drive. The owner of the car dealership would emphasize the significance of this step with the reminder, "You have to make them orgasm." The customer's delight with the car should lead him or her to want to be able to drive it every day. Frank felt that the demonstration drive was an opportune time to ask critical questions. While concentrating on driving the new car, the customer was less likely to embellish the truth than when just sitting in a chair in the office.

Another opportunity for seizing control offered itself when the customer wanted to trade in his or her car. It was important that the salesperson was in full view of the customer as he assessed the trade-in. Any small blemish would receive a gentle touching or rubbing from the salesperson's hand. If a tire seemed worn, the salesman would squat down and gently rub his hand over it without saying a word. The goal of this procedure was to degrade the customer's trade-in vehicle without being offensive or threatening. The silent recognition of the blemishes caused customers to feel bad about their car, but they did not feel the need to defend themselves or their car. It usually brought them closer to making a deal.

Now it's time for the "payment bump"—the salesperson quickly figures the best-case payment scenario and adds an amount of about $100 to $150, asking customers what size of monthly payments they were looking for, "$400 or $450 a month?" If the customer is planning to pay $250 a month but is too embarrassed to say so, having heard the higher figure of $450, the customer would be more likely to say $300 or so, which is what the salesperson had originally calculated. During these negotiations, the customer in his or her mind begins to establish a personal relationship with the selected automobile. To strengthen the customer's growing relationship to the car, the sales person may at this point mention that they only have one or two of this particular vehicle in stock and getting another one in the color preferred by the customer will be difficult because of the heavy demand at the manufacturer's. Thus, the principle of scarcity, discussed in greater detail in the next chapter, can be used as an instrument of persuasion.

While the purchase papers are being drawn up in the automobile dealership, the customer has time to increase the psychological commitment to the new shiny car. As the customer imagines the thrill of driving the new car, the sales person returns after having discussed the purchase with the supervisor and sadly informs the customer that the supervisor did not approve of the low price. Even though the salesperson promised to forego part of the sales commission, the supervisor insists that the quoted price is much too low. Quite often, the customer who has made the commitment under the influence of the low-ball price will purchase the car at a higher price (Cialdini, 2001).

There are times when a customer might get upset after disclosure of the deal and might get up and walk out. The seasoned salesperson never gets up at this point; he remains seated while attempting to calm down the customer and gently invites him or her to sit down again. On rare occasions, customers may storm out the door, but they usually have to return because their car keys are still in the hands of the salesperson from having assessed the value of the trade-in. Those are just some of the "control points" in the automobile business. Frank ought to know; he was promoted to sales manager and put in charge of training dozens of new salespeople.

This example of business proceedings in an automobile dealership has included quite a number of persuasion techniques used by the sales personnel in order to control the customer's decisions. Not every one of the described techniques will be applied in every one of the dealerships' car sales and, by the same token, the list of strategies described here is by no means complete. Inventive marketers will continue to provide new approaches to controlling consumers' actions for years to come.

※ Paychecks Demanding Loyalty

Although labor unions have exerted control on industry, most people working for a living would probably say that employers hold the most control and power in the work world. Certainly the issuing of paychecks is a symbol of control because the recipient of the paycheck is bound to perform certain work activities for a determined length of time. However, the paycheck demands more than that; loyalties and team spirit are just a few of the concepts expected in exchange for the money. Until recently, in some parts of the world employees identified strongly with the company they were working for, to the point where it became a matter of individual pride. People have a great need to identify with organizations. Employers make it seem a privilege for the employee to work for them. Employees' loyalties can increase a company's productivity and can create an innovative work atmosphere.

In the past, workers in coal mines, steel mills, and other branches of industry suffered injuries related to their physically dangerous work activities. Many of the workers did not blame or sue their employers for the damage done to their bodies. The risks of injury were a silent part of the work agreement, the loyalty to the paycheck, and the expectation that the employer would somehow take care of them. The workers were aware of the danger they were exposed to in their daily work. They had heard of others before them who had sustained serious injuries while fulfilling their job responsibilities.

Loyalties can literally be carried to one's deathbed, as in the case of Dr. Hosokawa, a chemist with the Japanese Chisso Corporation. In 1907 the small Japanese town of Minamata had encouraged the Chisso Corporation to move there and provide jobs for the population of the town. Until then their main source of income had been fishing, but the corporation dumped waste into Minamata Bay, which caused damage to the fishing areas. In the mid-1950s, people noticed domestic animals dying and local residents developing a disease that seemed to be mercury poisoning.

Although in 1956, a Chisso chemist blamed the disease on the population's diet of fish from Minamata Bay, the company continued dumping waste into the water. Three years later independent researchers determined that the Chisso Corporation's mercury discharges caused the disease, and a Chisso chemist attempted to demonstrate the truth. The company management, however, concealed his findings and prevented him from conducting further experiments. Although aware of the danger that came from the company's mercury discharges, he kept his silence for many years until 1973, when on his deathbed he finally disclosed the whole story (Schwartz & Gibb, 1999).

In cases like that, loyalty becomes just another term for being controlled. The employees' loyalty and team spirit can be expected to have developed out of cooperative personal values, but employers who demand the degree of loyalty described above clearly operate out of competitive values and beliefs.

There were times in the history of American automobile manufacturers when employees did not dare drive a foreign made car to work and leave it on the company's parking lot. Loyalty for the particular manufacturer's product meant purchasing their cars—after all that's what their paycheck and the company's discount was all about. It wasn't just the leadership of the carmaker that frowned on the sight of foreign built cars; coworkers apparently also took a strong dislike to their colleagues who demonstrated impaired loyalty to their employer. Interestingly, those who damaged their coworkers' foreign automobiles were never caught, even though it happened in broad daylight.

Loyalty, however, becomes a questionable variable when companies make use of another tool of control, the pink slip. In order to remain competitive and to meet the stockholders' expectations, corporate restructurings have been translated into significant reductions in the number of employees. Workforce reduction creates anxiety in those who have not yet received their pink slip (Garten, 2001). While the threat of losing one's job can increase motivation to work harder, it can also have a demoralizing effect—especially when at the same time outsized CEOs leave the company with large severance packages. After experiencing the stress of the uncertainty, employees may finally cease to care about their jobs or the company. In that case neither the paycheck nor the pink slip is an effective tool of control anymore.

In colleges and universities, faculty holds control over students' grades—and to some degree—over the students' future, but the students also exert control over faculty when they complete their faculty evaluation forms. For some, this is the time for revenge and for exerting control over the granting of the teacher's tenure and professorship.

▓ Controlling with Brand Names

The fashion industry has long been associated with controlling a part of the population by having logos or trademarks visibly attached to their products, thus making them a status symbol for the owner to proudly display. Wearing a certain brand of shirt or shoes or carrying a particular handbag announces to the world that the owner enjoys an elevated standing in the social order, backed by financial resources. Traditionally, the target market for the fashion industry consisted of adult women with money. Today the market has expanded to include men, young people, and people with less money, those who buy shirts, underwear, or sport shoes among other things. The particular sports shoe has become a status symbol, which is not confined to the sports arena but is now displayed on the streets, in schools and colleges, in restaurants, and even in places of business (Schwartz & Gibb, 1999). The endorsements of public figures, such as Michael Jordan, Peyton Manning, or—until the scandal broke about his personal life—Tiger Woods, seem to communicate to the public that in order to become successful, it is necessary to be seen wearing or carrying the items or articles of clothing endorsed by the celebrities. The Tiger Woods scenario raises an interesting question: "How to accurately estimate one's power?" Who is immune to public opinion and judgment? Did Mr. Woods believe that his personal indiscretions would not affect his selling power as he threw away his part of control over what the public is buying and with that negatively impacted his own financial status?

We are used to seeing brand names in stores and in advertising; we may even search for particular brands that have received high ratings for quality or price in the consumer literature. There is, however, a whole other area where certain brands exercise control. Businesses, who sell exclusively through home parties, are based on ladders of control. Perhaps one of the oldest and best known of these businesses is the Tupperware organization. Going back to 1956, the company guide to organizing Tupperware parties explained, as quoted by Don Herzog (2006, p. 153): "The whole party plan . . . is built on the basic needs of human beings. People need to express themselves. And one of the best ways of doing it is by putting on a Tupperware party." The prospective Tupperware representative/dealer who is being recruited "seems like a mindless pawn in a corporate game or, to ratchet up the rhetoric, like a proletarian who's relieved the capitalist of the burden of having to exploit her by learning how to exploit and even colonize herself" (p. 154). For the good of the family, Tupperware indicated that when all family members are engaged in the project, the product could serve as a family-bonding kit.

At occasions, such as Tupperware parties, the principle of liking comes into play. While officially the salesperson might be regarded as the persuader, in reality the host or hostess who has invited a circle of friends to the party is a strong source of influence here. Because the friends like the host or hostess, they are more likely to purchase items in this setting than if they were meeting the salesperson in a neutral environment. Unfortunately, there are no statistics available about the number of people who have abstained from purchasing an item after attending a Tupperware party. It takes a person of strong mind and character to resist the entreaty of the hostess (who is usually a good friend of the guest) and the representative or dealer to leave the party without a purchase.

Of course, the dealer would be the first to loudly and clearly refute the idea of "entreaty"—nevertheless that is exactly what it is. Most people are too polite not to buy an item or two, especially after having partaken in some of the offered refreshments and let's not forget the guest is very likely to encounter the hostess again because they travel in the same circles; otherwise she would not have been invited in the first place. By not buying, the guest would let the hostess down—perhaps even reduce the size of the "hostess gift."

Tupperware was an early company in this type of business, but numerous others have followed the lead. There are home parties for ladies' lingerie, cosmetics, silver jewelry, arts and crafts items, and many more. Some of them have taken to quietly displaying the offered items in elegant showcases and discreet placement of prices or pricelists. "The product speaks for itself, so there is never a formal presentation or sales talk" is the promise announced on the invitation, and ". . . by all means, bring a guest or two" is the implication. The façade may look different but the underlying principle is the same. Those who are friends of the hostess or the dealer have options they can exercise: Attend the party and buy an item they may or may not need or stay away. But as mentioned earlier, most likely they will meet again and it can make for an awkward meeting. Are the hostesses and dealers aware of the control they are exerting over their friends and acquaintances? If they are, their ready answer is "There is no sales talk, nobody has to buy anything. It's just a friendly get-together."

Some companies offer their dealers income not only from the products they sell but also through recruitment activities. For instance, Amway dealers earn their serious money by recruiting new dealers and receiving a cut on their sales and on the sales of the dealers recruited by the first recruited dealers. Apparently, this goes on and on in perpetuity, so the more generations of dealers one recruits, the more money one makes. However, the dealers cannot retire from selling the product themselves, no matter how high they rise within the organization they still have to close a certain number of sales every month (Herzog, 2006). In order to become a dealer in these companies, individuals have to purchase a pricey demonstration kit from the corporation. Thus goes the control through all the rungs of the ladder.

A different kind of brand name organization can be understood in some church associations. A recent press release from the office of the Indiana secretary of state (Rokita, 2009) focused on charges brought against a former pastor and his three sons who allegedly targeted their victims through their faith, committing affinity fraud. According to court documents, the father and three sons exploited their victims' religious convictions in attempts to conceal their elaborate Ponzi scheme from potential investors. The investors were duped into purchasing bonds that raised at least $120 million with the announced purpose that the bonds were to finance church construction and expansion.

The four men created an umbrella company for their scheme that produced training materials for those church members who were encouraged to sell bonds to their fellow church members. The training materials instructed the church members to start a sales call with a prayer and quote Bible scriptures throughout the sales calls, and, above all, "[to] never sell the facts, sell warm stewardship and the Lord" (Trigg, 2009, p. 1), somewhat reminiscent of the home parties where the real sales product is displayed quietly without sales talk. Apparently, the Lord and the quotes from the Bible, along with the prayer, represented a powerful influence on the faithful church members to the tune of $120 million.

Well-known brand names often carry the aura of authority and people's belief in authorities opens the doors to persuasion approaches that include the mere trappings of authority, be it in clothing and outward appearance or an actor performing in a certain role. Those old enough to remember seeing the actor Robert Young playing a physician on the TV program "Marcus Welby, M.D." may also remember Robert Young's successful advertising career, advising the public against caffeine in commercials for decaffeinated Sanka coffee and extolling the benefits of Camel cigarettes (Cialdini, 1993).

■ Opposing Goals and Conflicting Values in Family Enterprises

When two different sets of values and control systems are combined and intertwined in a person's life because the individual's work world is a family business, the situation can become complicated. According to the American Family Business Survey, a study conducted by the Raymond Institute, family businesses account for 64 percent of the U.S. gross domestic product. About 39 percent of chief executive officers at these family-owned businesses plan to retire within five years; many of those have not yet chosen a successor. Transferring family businesses to the younger generation will generate a lot of business activity in the future, and given those facts, a significant power shift can be expected in the world of family-owned businesses (Wall, 2003).

However, other more competitive activities can be expected as well, because family loyalties and business sense do not always operate on similar levels. Rivalries within families for the most powerful positions in the business can result in bitter feuds between different factions within one family, impacting both the business and the family relationships.

In the book of *Genesis*, the Bible presents several accounts of rivalries within families, starting with Cain killing his brother Abel because he was angry that God had accepted Abel's gifts but refused Cain's gifts (*Living Bible*, 1971). Of the twin boys born to Isaac and Rebekah, Jacob, the younger, made his older brother Esau sell him in exchange for a meal the birthright of being the older and—with the help of his mother—tricked their father Isaac into bestowing upon Jacob the blessings reserved for the older son. Jacob's favorite son was Joseph; out of envy his brothers wanted to kill him but sold him to traders who took him to Egypt. Evidently, competition for the better or more powerful position has been with us from the beginning of time.

Murder, betrayal, and adultery are still very much a part of our world, and neither religious nor mythical laws nor the laws of humans seem to be able to control the forces of evil—perhaps because, as James Frey (2000, p. 38) stated, "[T]he God of obedience has become the God of freedom. Our heroes don't follow the law; they can only succeed if they disobey it. Our cultural values are individualist, not tribal." It has become a case of individual interests above community interests and of the end justifying the means.

Not all conflicting values in family enterprises are resolved through murder, adultery, and betrayal—although betrayal is a frequent factor, especially when competition is encouraged. The patriarch, who inherited the family business by successfully competing with his siblings for the powerful position, may honestly believe that competition strengthens those who compete. He may therefore pass on the tradition of competition to his own children, thinking he is helping each one of them to grow stronger mentally and economically.

William, the proud owner of a chain of furniture stores knew the recipe; with good reason, his siblings gave him the nickname "The Conqueror." William and Hanna, his wife, had three children, Jonathan, Annette, and Pete. Pete, being addicted to alcohol and drugs since his high school days, had left the family compound to live somewhere in California. His father had disinherited him with the provision that if he sobered up, he would give him a second chance, but he didn't tell him what the second chance would be.

Jonathan, the oldest, now a man in his early 30s was neither handsome nor ugly; unremarkable would have been the word to describe his appearance if it had not been for his sad hazel eyes. Jonathan worked in his father's furniture store. As long as he could remember, he wanted to be a comedian although or because of the fact that his school years were marked by painful shyness. Jonathan believed that if he could hide behind a role, he would be able to overcome his shyness and people would overlook his shortcomings. Comedians did not have to compete with the football stars for the girls' attention; comedians were not in competition with any glamorous man.

Annette, 16 months younger than Jonathan, was gregarious and excelled in sports. William often remarked that it was a shame that Annette could not be a boy; she had all the qualities required to run the family business. Jonathan did not measure up to his father's expectations of what his son and heir should be. Despite his longing for the stage, Jonathan followed his father's demands to enter the furniture business. A brief apprenticeship in cabinetry and furniture repair combined with a two-year degree in business was his father's plan for him. Jonathan complied.

While his father kept him busy in the store, Jonathan managed to work on a few comedy routines and was able to obtain a Friday night booking at a local nightclub. His act was well received, although it needed polishing. The owner of the club actually encouraged Jonathan to continue working on his routine, and he offered him another spot on Saturday nights. Jonathan was elated. He felt that he had finally found an avenue to express himself and to be recognized. However, his father did not share in the excitement; he was furious. How dare Jonathan make a fool of himself and embarrass the family. Their customers would make fun of them all. The store's integrity was at stake. Buying furniture was a serious undertaking for people. It required a stable, trustworthy, and dignified atmosphere; it was not a joking matter. Either Jonathan would quit his "foolishness" at once or he was no longer an accepted member of the family.

Jonathan capitulated and focused all his efforts on the business. His girlfriend Susie was disappointed in Jonathan's giving in and giving up. She broke up with him, knowing that Jonathan had deserted himself. However, William's trust in his oldest son was shaken; he removed decision-making responsibilities from Jonathan and treated him worse than a hired worker, demanding overtime work for no extra pay.

William insisted that the whole family meet for dinner every Friday evening. He used the time to discuss the business and plans for the next week as well as future plans. Missing a Friday dinner meeting was an unpardonable sin, not to be committed lightly. One of William's control schemes was to discuss matters important to the missing person if anyone dared not show up. He also instructed everybody present not to "gossip" or discuss the information with the member who had been absent. By keeping the absent family member in the dark about the ongoing business, William was making sure that everybody attended. Annette took her father's demands seriously. She also realized that her father would put his trust in her if she did not disappoint him. If her brother wanted to take that risk, she was not about to interfere, especially if it enhanced her position. The cost of missing a Friday dinner was too high; it was almost impossible to recover from such an affront.

Annette had recently married Bert, an ambitious young man, who had made quite an impression on William. At the wedding, William announced that he had invited Bert to join the family business. Jonathan was surprised to hear the news; nothing like that had been mentioned at the family dinners. One day in the storage room in back of the furniture store Jonathan noticed that a group of office furniture had been put aside in one corner of the store with a sign stating that these items were not to be sold. They were intended for Bert's use. Jonathan feared that his father was providing Bert with an office instead of advancing Jonathan to the manager's position. Apparently, once again his father had made decisions about the business without consulting him or even informing him about it before the decision was exercised.

As it turned out, Bert was to become the manager of a new store in a different part of town, while Jonathan remained in the main store—under his father's thumb. Bert (and Annette) had received the promotion to greater independence that Jonathan had hoped for. His one-night stand as a comedian had cost him plenty. Bert and Annette were now openly competing with him—and apparently successfully so. Financially he was dependent on his job in the family business. With his knowledge of the furniture business and his repair skills he could work for another company; however, joining the competition would be an even greater sin than missing Friday night dinner. He might as well die or leave the country.

William, with the assistance of his powerless wife Hanna, had set the stage for an atmosphere of power for him and fear, distrust, betrayal, and competition for the rest of the family, which pervaded the family and the business.

▓ Competition—All in the Family

In the 20th century, Dorothy Buffum Chandler, the wife of the third publisher of the *Los Angeles Times*, Norman Chandler, was an ardent fundraiser for a music center for Los Angeles county. During the nine years of her fund drive on behalf of the Music Center she collected $19 million in private donations. One might say that this was a worthwhile undertaking for the benefit of the community. Her arm-twisting techniques in extracting great sums of money from the famous and wealthy have been described as breathtaking (McDougal, 2001). She refused donations that in her opinion were not large enough and blackmailed or shamed her victims until their contributions met her standards for what was appropriate for her ambitious goal. She used the *Times* to report on her successes and for her threats and arm-twisting techniques—all for her own aggrandizement.

Dorothy Chandler's obsession with fund raising did not stop at the family threshold; she competed fiercely and ruthlessly with her own daughter for monetary contributions. The Los Angeles County Museum of Art was the cultural cause adopted by her daughter Camilla. Camilla's mother openly sabotaged her daughter's fund-raising efforts. Dorothy went so far as to threaten firing the managing editor of the *Los Angeles Times* for reporting on Camilla's fund-raising activities if it was done before her own goal had been completely accomplished. Her reasoning was that Los Angeles "needed Mozart and Puccini far more desperately than Renoir and Picasso . . . so she pulled out all the stops to defeat her daughter. . . . She could absolutely destroy people if they didn't do what she wanted them to do" (McDougal, 2001, p. 242).

Perhaps Dorothy Buffum Chandler's behavior could not be classified as an act of betrayal, although her daughter might have considered it as such. It was, however, a fierce competition, controlled by Dorothy that had Dorothy's aggrandizement as a goal. When it came to the decision as to what methods to use to reach her goal, Dorothy did not hesitate to seize control of the situation to defeat her daughter's work.

The dynamics in William's story in the previous section shows similarities to the report of the Chandler family. William did not think twice about diminishing his children's self-confidence if they did not exactly follow his orders, and by setting the parameters for the competition between Jonathan and Annette, he laid the groundwork for the likely defeat of one of the siblings.

▓ Guessing and Mind Reading in the Pursuit of Business Advantages

In business as well as in interpersonal situations that invite the seizing of control, people try to outguess one another about the others' goals and plans. "Mind reading facilitates deception, and deception encourages mind reading. If one organism knows what another is after, if it is able to divine its mood and second-guess its reactions, this opens the door for exploitation and manipulation," observed philosophy professor David Livingstone Smith (2004, p. 35).

Was it mind reading when, in the 19th century, the American robber baron Jay Gould set up a company that threatened the monopoly of the telegraph company Western Union? Some time after Western Union spent a lot of money to buy Gould's company Gould created another company in competition with Western Union. Again, Western Union purchased the second company to keep Gould from competing. When Gould started a third company, Western Union believed that Gould wanted to be bought out again, and they were unprepared for the takeover struggle that Gould started and that ended with his gaining complete control over Western Union. The pattern of starting competing businesses deceived Western Union into expecting that Gould would continue this practice. However, while collecting large sums of money along the way, Gould finally did the opposite of what Western Union anticipated.

Was it Gould's original plan to control Western Union's thought processes in developing the buy-out pattern? The series of events would indicate that he did, or perhaps the idea occurred to him as a consequence of the first or even just the second buy-out. Whatever his original plans might have been, he seized the opportunity to put himself in complete control.

An ability to read minds can be useful in protection against manipulation. "Mind reading and manipulation bounce off each other in an intimate dialectic spiraling" (Smith, 2004, p. 35); however, Western Union did not master the skill as well as Gould had done at the time of their competition.

For those who have not developed their mind-reading skills sufficiently, there are other ways of impairing the opponent's judgment and decision-making abilities (Goldstein, Martin, & Cialdini, 2008). For instance, any emotionally charged issue, regardless whether it produces positive or negative feelings, leads people to become less sensitive to differences in the magnitude of numbers. Under the influence of emotions, people are more likely to pay attention to the simple presence or absence of an event as opposed to the specific numbers that characterize the event, that is, people are more likely to pay attention to the simple presence or absence of an emotion-laden offer than to distinguish among the details of the offer.

Therefore, in any high-value decision-making situation leading to strong emotional arousal, it would be good practice to allow a period of time to pass, for composing oneself. In business, people often schedule meetings back to back as a matter of convenience, or so they say. However, scheduling short breaks between decision-making meetings will significantly reduce the likelihood that the feelings generated by an emotionally charged meeting will spill over into the next. Especially, if the second meeting is one that requires budget or purchasing decisions, entering the meeting in a calm state of mind will facilitate the appropriateness of the decisions.

As discussed in Chapters 3 and 4, the knowledge of individuals' emotional responses can be used to control those individuals' thought and behavior. Pushing people's "anger buttons" can have the effect of distracting them from the goals they originally wanted to pursue. However, according to Goldstein, Martin, and Cialdini mentioned above, any strong emotions, positive or negative, will influence what aspects of an issue the individuals experiencing these emotions at the time are most likely to pay attention to. The more stressed the individuals are by their strong emotions, the simpler the aspects of an issue under discussion they will attend to. The more complicated aspects—and those are probably the more important ones—will receive less concentrated—if any attention. If those who are seeking to influence others' decisions and actions recognize the importance different moods play, so should the ones who feel controlled by the actions of others be cognizant of this significant aspect.

6 ▪ ▪ ▪

Marketing for Control

Advertising has much in common with politics: Control of the public through the tools of propaganda, persuasion, and packaging. They have the same target: The public, called consumers or voters, depending on who the control-seeking agent is. They want to influence the public by affecting several different kinds of emotions. They employ similar tools and techniques; in fact, people in politics increasingly make use of techniques that have proven to be successful in advertising. Persuasion and propaganda have been with us for a long time, whereas the idea of packaging, as distinguished from the action of placing a product in a package, is relatively new.

To accommodate advertising and politics on a grand scale, a whole new industry has been created. The mass media is the primary vehicle for displaying the persuasion, propaganda, and packaging efforts of the control-seeking agents to the public (Pratkanis & Aronson, 2001).

According to the dictionary, the word persuade means to move by argument, entreaty, or expostulation to a belief, position, or course of action. The term propaganda has the meaning of the spreading of ideas, information, or rumor for the purpose of helping or injuring an institution, a cause, or a person. Ideas, facts, or allegations spread deliberately to further one's cause or to damage an opposing cause are parts of propaganda. The meanings of the two terms, persuasion and propaganda, overlap because in its broadest meaning propaganda is a form of persuasion.

▦ Propaganda

Considering the different facets of propaganda, one is reminded of the distinction between propaganda and education offered more than five decades ago by the psychologist Max Wertheimer, a refugee from Nazi Germany (Pratkanis & Aronson, 2001). In Wertheimer's view, propaganda attempts to keep people from thinking independently and acting as humans with rights (Luchins & Luchins, 1978, p. 277). Propaganda manipulates people's emotions and prejudices to impose the propagandist's will on them. In contrast, education is meant to provide the skills for people to think for themselves and make their own decisions. Education should encourage critical thinking. Propaganda with its emotional appeals makes use of a long list of techniques in attempting to influence our attitudes and actions.

In its relatively short existence, the word propaganda has seen several changes in its meaning. Its first appearance seems to have occurred in 1622, in the wake of the Protestant Reformation, when Pope Gregory XV established the papal propaganda office with the purpose of coordinating efforts to convince people to "voluntarily" accept church doctrines. In the Catholic countries, the word was used with a positive connotation, being similar in meaning to education or preaching; but in Protestant areas the word was given a negative connotation (Pratkanis & Aronson, 2001).

With the beginning of the 20th century, the word propaganda came to mean persuasion tactics applied during World War I and was later used by totalitarian governments. More recently, the meaning of the word has changed to describe techniques used to influence the masses through suggestion and manipulation of words and symbols that play on people's emotions. The goal of propaganda activity is to convince individuals to accept voluntarily the suggested beliefs and attitudes as their own.

As master of propaganda, the acknowledged father of public relations, Edward L. Bernays, was instrumental in convincing women to smoke and in convincing American families to start the day with a hearty breakfast consisting of eggs and, particularly, bacon (Held, 2009). In his media campaign created to shape public opinion, Bernays applied psychoanalytic principles to public relations and advertising. Through his uncle, the father of psychoanalysis, Sigmund Freud, Bernays was introduced to the notion that irrational forces drive human behavior. He rose to the challenge of using these irrational forces to sell his clients' products. Lagging sales of bacon, one of their main meat products, troubled the Beechnut Packing Company when Bernays came to the rescue.

Bernays' question of who influences the public regarding their food consumption led him to approach physicians for their opinion. Would they recommend a light or a hearty breakfast? The physicians overwhelmingly endorsed a hearty breakfast. Publicizing these "findings" in a marketing campaign put bacon and eggs on the American breakfast table.

In his 1928 book *Propaganda* Bernays suggested that understanding the group mind provided possibilities of manipulating people's behavior without their awareness of it, and he delivered the proof. At that time it was not acceptable for women to smoke in public unless they wanted to be thought of as being sexually permissive. Nevertheless, the president of the American Tobacco Company, George Washington Hill, a Bernays client, wanted to broaden the market for the Lucky Strike cigarette brand by turning women into smokers.

In consultation with New York's leading psychoanalyst, Dr. A. A. Brill, Bernays learned that in women's view, cigarettes were a symbol of male power. Associating women's smoking with a challenge to male power became the foundation of Lucky Strike's "Torches of Freedom" campaign, which was unveiled in New York's 1929 annual Easter Parade. Approaching the editor of *Vogue* magazine, Bernays received a list of debutantes who were led to believe that they would be helping the growth of women's rights by smoking cigarettes in the most public of places, Fifth Avenue. For sufficient coverage of the "Torches of Freedom Parade" the press received the information beforehand.

Bernays' notion that associating products with people's emotions would cause them to behave in irrational ways was confirmed. Connecting smoking and women's rights promoted a feeling of independence, while in reality women were not having any more freedom than they had without smoking. Nevertheless, linking smoking to women's rights has been successful, being used again in 1968 by the Philip Morris Company when they introduced their Virginia Slims brand of cigarettes. Marketing of this narrower and longer brand of cigarettes as a female-oriented spin-off to their Benson and Hedges brand, Philip Morris used the slogan "You've come a long way, baby" and targeted their campaign to young professional women. San Francisco, California, was chosen as the first test market, and the campaign was originally scheduled to last six months, but because of the enormous success the campaign was cut short after six weeks (Wikipedia 2009a).

The basic themes in marketing campaigns for Virginia Slims have been independence, liberation, emancipation, slimness, style, and glamour—generally in contrast to ads for men's cigarettes. Well-known models and designer fashions were featured in television and print ads. During the 1970s and early 1980s the growth of women's tennis was linked to the Virginia Slims–sponsored Women's Tennis Association Tour. Although like other cigarette brands, Virginia Slims' popularity has declined and the brand is no longer heavily promoted, its brand loyalty is still one of the highest in the industry.

Not often has the investment of a box of Havana cigars brought such great dividends. When Bernays presented the cigars to his uncle, Sigmund Freud reciprocated with a copy of his *General Introductory Lectures,* which apparently stimulated Bernays to apply psychoanalytic principles to the field of advertising in order to manipulate the public's emotions and to control their purchasing behaviors. The legacy of Edward Bernays was passed on to—among many others—the Leo Burnett advertising agency, which handled the Virginia Slims account. The agency is still alive and well today.

▓ Persuasion

Although there is overlap between the two terms, historically not all persuasion has been propaganda. The ancient Greeks and Romans used rhetorical techniques to develop discourse for explaining and clarifying an issue. Debates, arguments, and discussions were used to persuade listeners against or in favor of the speaker's position on the issue. Persuasion then had a function of educating the audience. Today, with messages bombarding the individual from all sides, there is not enough time to persuade through lengthy debates. Today, the message has to impact individuals immediately, and persuasion, in order to be effective and successful, had to employ different methods.

How does persuasion work? Social scientists have suggested this explanation: In the 18th century, Franz Anton Mesmer claimed that he could control human behavior by passing a magnet over a person's body, with the effect of redirecting the flow of the animal fluid within the body. Hypnotic trance and spiritual healing were further steps in the attempts of achieving cures of all sorts of physical and psychological ailments. Hypnotic trance states with subliminal commands are still in vogue in some circles, and crystals have replaced the magnets of old.

However, hypnosis is not a guaranteed tool for controlling others because not everybody is susceptible to being hypnotized. For instance, among college students, about 30 percent show high susceptibility to hypnosis, whereas 40 percent have low susceptibility, and the remaining 30 percent fall somewhere in between, with medium susceptibility to hypnosis (Plotnik, 2002). Those who are more responsive to being hypnotized actually expect to be put into a trance state and cooperate with the suggestions made by the hypnotist. Rather than being under the power of a hypnotist, subjects choose to respond to suggestions or—in congruence with the discussion in Chapter 1—are controlled by their own expectations.

How to influence people is of utmost importance in business. Customer research experts spend time and money to find out how to sell ideas to various types of decision makers. In a survey of almost 1,700 executives five different types of decision makers could be distinguished (Miller, Williams, & Hayashi, 2004). There are the charismatics, who become excited about new ideas but need to depend on others for investigating the details. Thinkers work through each pro and con of every option by themselves before making a decision. Most difficult to persuade are the skeptics, who are suspicious of every piece of information, distrusting anything that does not match their worldview. Followers are people who base their decisions on what others whom they trust have chosen in the past. For controllers, it is important that they are in charge of every aspect of the decision-making process. The persuader would have to convince them that the ideas involved are their own.

Sociologists have warned that people have become vulnerable to persuasion because of today's social isolation that deprives us of community spirit and communal relationships. In their isolated existence, people become easy targets for persuasive influences of the media.

▓ Psychological Principles as a Basis for Control

Those who wanted to believe in the possibility that human beings could be controlled through outside forces found a fertile ground in psychology. The behaviorist John Watson (1924) believed that with the systematic application of the principles of classical conditioning, developed by Ivan Pavlov, any infant taken at birth could be shaped into any type of human being desired. In the late 19th century, E. L. Thorndike (1898), on the basis of his animal experiments, pronounced the law of effect, which states that behaviors followed by positive consequences will be strengthened in the organism, whereas behaviors followed by negative consequences will be weakened.

Some 30 years later B. F. Skinner (1938) analyzed ongoing behaviors of animals in his laboratory and found Thorndike's law of effect useful but insisted that in order to analyze ongoing behaviors one needed objective ways for measuring them. Skinner proposed as a unit of behavior an operant response, which is a response that can be modified by its consequences and is a meaningful unit of ongoing behavior that can be easily measured. By measuring or recording operant responses, an animal's ongoing reactions during learning could be analyzed. Skinner called this kind of learning operant conditioning, which focuses on how consequences (rewards or punishments) affect behaviors.

Although one might be tempted to declare that these developments laid the foundation for the manipulation and control of human beings by other human beings, exploration and development of theories have not stopped at the behaviorist orientation. Proponents of cognitive learning theories, such as Albert Bandura (1986), in his social cognitive theory, emphasized the importance of observation, imitation, and self-reward in the development and learning of social skills and many other behaviors. Unlike operant and classical conditioning, Bandura's theory states that it is not necessary to perform any observable behaviors or receive any external rewards in order to learn. During social cognitive learning, attention, memory, imitation, and motivation are the major processes in operation.

Considering the utilitarian value of psychological theories to those who work in the field of persuasion, the classical conditioning and operant conditioning approaches would be irrelevant because the target is not considered to be a passive entity that only responds to reward and punishment. Instead, the target is an active participant expected to make decisions. It is the decision-making process that the persuasive forces are focused on. With increasing inventiveness and sophistication, the persuaders will develop and implement techniques that will be directed at individuals' attention, memory, and tendency for imitation in order to trigger the desired kind of motivation and obtain the desired behaviors.

▓ Techniques of Persuasion

Persuasion is a deliberate attempt to influence people's attitudes and behaviors in situations where they have choices rather than being confined to only one path. Because of a range of alternatives available to the individual, persuaders rely on several techniques. Influence techniques that are organized around seven principles have been identified (Cialdini, 1993). The principle of contrast builds on the sequencing of message or stimuli presentation. For instance, one's wife or girlfriend might appear less attractive after just having watched a Miss America contest.

Another technique is to rely on the principle of reciprocity (similar to ingratiating behaviors described in Chapter 3). It is basically the act of doing a favor for somebody who then feels obligated to return the favor. In business it often takes the form of giving free samples; cult members have used this technique in handing flowers to people on the street to get their attention and good will.

A variation of this rule is the door-in-the-face technique. Here the persuader makes a large request on another person, which will be refused. Then the persuader returns with a much smaller request, which will most likely be met with agreement because the target person feels guilty over the first refusal. The second, much smaller, request is actually what the persuader wanted all along. Another variation often seen in sales is the that's-not-all technique (Zimbardo & Leippe, 1991). The persuader offers a certain deal to a person, but before the person can respond with an acceptance or rejection, the persuader throws in an additional item that makes the original offer appear even more desirable. It is important to add the item before the target person has a chance to utter a rejection. Having made a public statement, people are more reluctant to change their minds. If they have not verbalized the "no" yet, they don't lose face by saying "yes" and agreeing to the deal.

Cialdini's (1993) principle of consistency, and what is sometimes called the rule of commitment, presents another powerful persuasion approach using different techniques and making use of people's tendency to wanting to appear consistent and not to be thought of as fickle. This approach may build on small commitments at the beginning. For instance, in the foot-in-the-door technique the persuader first makes a small request, one that is difficult to refuse because of its smallness. However, by agreeing with the small request the target person has made a mental or emotional commitment. Psychological pressure comes to play on the person when the persuader follows up with a larger request.

Another variation of the commitment rule found to operate in sales is the so-called low-ball technique, mentioned in the previous chapter within the context of automobile dealership sales techniques. Product testimonials from satisfied customers and canned laughter on TV sitcoms are examples of the social proof principle, carrying the implication that what other people think is correct. The principle of liking operates in businesses that sell their products in home sales, such as Tupperware parties of old, where the salesperson may be regarded as the persuader but in reality the host or hostess who has invited a circle of friends to the party is a strong source of influence. Because the friends like the host or hostess, they are more likely to purchase items in this setting than if they were meeting the salesperson in a neutral environment.

The principle of scarcity represents yet another approach of persuasion. Advertisements that include phrases such as "while supply lasts," "for a limited time only," or "only two left in stock, no rain checks" introduce a sense of urgency in the customer and plant the perception of scarcity in the customer's mind, which will propel him or her to visit the store immediately.

Those working in the advertising industry know the importance of appealing to people's reasoning styles, which are apt to change with the times. Where in the past the most impressive superlative claims about a product were made in their advertising materials, today a more sophisticated approach is applied. Keeping up with developing psychological research results, advertising techniques focus on more modest claims and declarations that appear to be verifiable.

On the other hand, incomplete comparison claims are still used to imply that a certain product is superior to others. To appear more open-minded, advertisers make use of the two-sided message, which gives the impression that they are honest enough to admit some negative aspect of the advertised product. Upon closer examination, the negative appearing aspect usually has no particular meaning relating to the product in question. For instance while pointing out all the positive features of a particular automobile, there may be a qualifier stating that there is no space for a wheelchair in the trunk or backseat, when in reality people buying that type of car would not be bothered with transporting anything like wheelchairs.

Persuasion works with people when they are actively thinking as well as when they are in a mindless state, but if persuasion is to be successful, the approaches are different for these two states. In the peripheral route, persuasion acts through simple cues. It could be the attractiveness of the communicator, whether or not people around the recipient agree or disagree with the position presented by the communicator or whether a reason is given to the recipient for complying with a request. In using the peripheral approach, the communicator or persuader assumes that the recipient will spend little attention and effort on processing the information. The promise of the message's success in the peripheral approach lies in the classic propaganda formula—delivery of a simple message that evokes a simple image, which plays on the emotions and prejudices of the recipient and elicits a clear response in the recipient.

In the central route, the recipient is thought to devote attention and thoughtful consideration to the true merits when the information is presented. The recipient may ask questions and raise arguments about the message. According to Richard Petty and John Cacioppo (1986), the success of this persuasion approach is a function of how well it can sustain its merit during the inquisition, which can turn out to be quite lengthy.

How would persuaders decide which approach to take with their message? We find the answer in the personal connection to the recipient or the target of the message. If the message holds great interest or importance for the target, the central approach would be the preferred one because it can be expected that the target will raise some questions, given the personal importance to the target. On the other hand, if there is only a tangential interest within the recipient, a simple statement of the message supported by well-known experts will be the most efficient route.

Those deliberations can work when the communicator is well acquainted with the personal background of the recipient. However, when the recipient or target audience includes large numbers of people, it is, of course, impossible to know individual backgrounds and preferences. In situations like that, and especially when the message is delivered through radio or television channels, the most reasonable approach would be the peripheral route, assuming that most people do not attend closely and are easily swayed by so-called expert opinions, and that is exactly what modern propaganda does.

Professional propagandists take advantage of the fact that most people do not devote careful thought to the messages directed at them but respond to simplistic persuasion techniques and limited reasoning

(Pratkanis & Aronson, 2001). In this situation it also helps that people are rationalizing creatures. If questioned later on why they responded in a decisive way to a message, most likely they will find many rational-sounding explanations to justify their actions. People have a tendency to explain to themselves and others why they made a certain decision or why they determined to behave in certain ways, because they have a need to appear logical and to protect their images of themselves.

Building on these observations, what are the main elements of influence used by successful persuaders? What is the message, and what is the best frame for it? These are important questions to be explored and answered. How an issue is being defined by the communicator can assist in achieving consent without even seeming to ask for it. The image of the persuader is of utmost importance. The persuader as the source of the message has to appear likeable and trustworthy. If the persuader seems honest, this lends credibility to the message. During the process of communication, the persuader carefully directs the targets' attention to what the communicator wants them to attend to and creates an atmosphere that arouses emotions in the targets. The target persons are encouraged to respond to their emotional state, rendering them preoccupied and more likely to comply with the message, as already discussed briefly in the previous chapter.

As noted at the beginning of this chapter, persuasion and propaganda overlap, and in some cases it is difficult to draw a clear line between them. Two guidelines for distinguishing between the two have been proposed (Pratkanis & Aronson, 2001): As the message is being communicated, (1) does it encourage or arouse thoughts about the issues mentioned or (2) does it discourage or eliminate any further thought processes?

Most messages elicit emotions in the target persons—what type of emotions and how does the communicator use them? Is the communicator mostly eliciting feelings of fear or deprecation? There may be the fear of being ridiculed if one does not agree with the message, or the target person may feel belittled in some way. Is the communicator bringing up feelings of encouragement or hope, perhaps through the use of flattery or of ambiguous hints of promises? This might make the target person feel special in some way and worthy of attention. Being aware of what happens to our cognitive processes and our emotional processes while under the influence of a particular communication will enable us to heed the signals our senses are receiving.

Emotions and moods impact people's thinking and reasoning, as do stress and fatigue affect people's ability to focus and concentrate. Perhaps nobody knew this better than the diplomat Klemens Wenzel Nepomuk Lothar von Metternich-Winneburg. Although born in Coblenz, Germany, he became the most influential player in the Austrian politics of the early 19th century. Facing Napoleon in a personal meeting on June 26, 1813, in the Marcolini Palace in Dresden, which lasted more than nine hours, Metternich kept up the pretense of neutrality while Napoleon pressed for Austria's full commitment to his cause (Age-of-the-Sage, 2009).

Napoleon's approach to his goal in the long meeting ranged from violent outbursts of fury to overly friendly persuasion tactics. Metternich, insisting on Austria's neutrality, remained calm even through Napoleon's fits of rage and threats. Napoleon's repeated threat, "We will meet in Vienna," only elicited Metternich's refusal to bargain.

Following Napoleon's eventual defeat in 1814, a great congress was arranged to convene at Vienna in the autumn of 1814. The Congress of Vienna became a lavish social festival during which diplomats and statesmen divided and reconstructed, amidst strong disagreements, the map of Europe, but Metternich's diplomatic talents persisted in exerting influence on the proceedings. His charm, determination, subtlety, and finesse played a major role in frustrating Russia's plans for annexation of Poland as well as Prussia's attempt to absorb Saxony. He succeeded in the development of a German Confederation under the leadership of Austria. Consequently, with Austria's influence on the Italian peninsula, its powers were greatly strengthened.

It has been said that in order to calm the contradictions created by the quarreling statesmen and to guide them toward his goals, Metternich ordered the courts' chefs to provide loads of pastries with tasty but heavy butter-cream fillings to be served as desserts during their midday meals. As expected by Metternich, the pastries were too seductive to be resisted, and the statesmen with their full stomachs were too tired to resist Metternich's directions toward his goals.

▩ The Indirect Technique of Self-Persuasion

In contrast to the traditional, direct techniques of persuasion described above, a highly effective, indirect technique is that of achieving self-persuasion within the targeted individuals (Aronson, 1999). People are placed in situations where they are motivated to persuade themselves to change their own attitudes or behavior. Reasons for choosing the more powerful and more long-lasting effects of self-persuasion strategies over direct techniques of persuasion include several factors. In direct persuasion, individuals often become aware of the fact that someone is attempting to influence them, whereas in self-persuasion, individuals strongly believe that the motivation for change originated within themselves.

Indirect persuasion has an enormous ally in social influence and its power. People have a tendency to conform to and comply with group behavior, without even being requested to do so. Publicized events, such as suicides of famous people or groups, bomb threats, UFO sightings, and airplane hijackings tend to appear in clusters. They *seem* to be contagious. Some behaviors, such as giggling or yawning, *are* contagious. Working on New York's Wall Street or London's Bond Street, males and females wear suits; on college campuses most students are dressed in blue jeans and shirts or sweaters. Even those who may be attempting to assert their individuality with different hairstyles and clothes often appear to be identifying themselves with others of the same microculture (Myers, 2005). However, most of the people, if asked for reasons, would express their beliefs that they made their choices independently.

Another reason for the effectiveness of self-persuasion lies in the fact that it relates to the unpleasant feelings that individuals experience when they do or say something that runs counter to their own beliefs. More than half a century ago, the theory of cognitive dissonance as developed by Leon Festinger (1957) stated that dissonance is experienced when an individual's actions and beliefs are incongruent or contradictory and threaten the individual's self-concept of being a rational person. To reduce the dissonance, people will do anything to bring those disparate cognitions into greater harmony.

An experiment in social psychology required volunteer subjects to undergo either a severe initiation or a mild initiation process to gain admission to a discussion group (Aronson, 1999). The group discussion itself was uninteresting and silly. As predicted, individuals who underwent the severe initiation persuaded themselves to find the discussion group more stimulating than the people who had gained admission relatively effortlessly. The individuals who had invested a lot going through the severe initiation process to gain admission were more likely to focus on the positive aspects of the group to reduce the dissonance within themselves for having spent that much effort for something of low value.

The experiment demonstrated how in conditions of high dissonance, individuals work hard to justify their attitudes and behaviors to themselves. Thus, in the most powerful persuasion strategy, that of self-persuasion, it is the to-be-persuaded individual who does the work of the persuader after the persuader has set the stage.

■ Packaging

Packaging has developed into an important industry in its own right. In the early 20th century, packages protected goods and ensured the safety of goods during transportation. Packages can be expressive by using different colors or printed directions on how to open them or how to use the item inside. As different materials and technologies developed, packages became relatively inexpensive to produce. The time had come to make use of the power of packages to sell products and control markets. The purpose of packaging was transformed from protection to promotion (Hine, 1993).

For the manufacturing industry, packaging is the final touch of a marketing campaign. It can bestow a powerful image on a product. Advertising and marketing consultants look to packaging as a way to reach customers' semiconscious realm of wants and expectations that have been shaped by the culture. The cosmetics industry is a prime example of manufacturing products that deal in dreams, illusions, and promises. Packaging is designed to evoke a particular mood for the product and the circumstances in which it is to be applied. Its promises seem unlimited, but they are never guaranteed. They are only implied.

It's not only wishes and desires that marketing efforts focus on: other—less joyous—emotions such as fear and guilt also lend themselves to controlling attempts. What working mother, with little time left for cooking meals from scratch, can resist the appeal of a frozen or otherwise partly prepared food? The food is depicted on the package in luscious colors of red and green for vegetables and juicy looking slices of meat. Guilt feelings about not always preparing balanced nutritious meals for her family will draw her to the item like a magnet.

The first law of advertising is to get the attention of the customer, which is to be followed by provoking action. The consumer, after having focused attention on the advertising, is expected to do something, namely buy the product. The customer's attention is then led on to another path, the guilt-inducing path: "If you don't buy this product, you will feel sorry!" Feelings of guilt propel the consumer into the action of purchasing.

Insurance companies have always been expert practitioners in applying guilt as the motivator that makes people buy their products. In the 1912 Travelers Insurance Company's advertising shame and blame are added to guilt in order to control the consumer. It is noted that there was no excuse for a man who would subject his wife to a future of poverty and privation because he did not purchase a life insurance policy (Goodrum & Dalrymple, 1990).

The design of a package can lead customers to believe that the product in this particular package is of higher quality than the same product in a package with a different design, as was demonstrated by marketing psychologist Louis Cheskin. In the final analysis "the package makes the final sales pitch, seals the commitment, and gets itself placed in the shopping cart. Advertising leads consumers into temptation. Packaging *is* the temptation. In many cases it is what makes the product possible" (Hine, 1993, p. 3).

▓ Image Packaging and Targets' Expectations

The idea of packaging has not been limited to marketing and advertising. Politics is another area where its potential value has been recognized. Similar to the tasks performed by market researchers for a given product, pollsters collect the opinions of voters and feed them back to the marketing experts who handle and package a specific political candidate. The well-packaged candidate projects an image that is honest, creditable, and stimulating without being threatening. The packaging must smooth out any contradictions, ambiguity, or other discomforting aspects in attempts to minimize the negative.

In the political arena, packaging is less concerned with the product itself (the candidate) than with the image (what good deeds is the candidate likely to do for the voter). Playing on the voters' expectations, image packaging is intended to influence how the candidate is perceived by the voters, not so much how the candidate really is. How much better the quality of life will be for the voter by supporting this candidate is the intended message. Those who remember the association made between former President John F. Kennedy and Alan Jay Lerner and Frederick Loewe's musical *Camelot*, which was an adaptation from the T. H. White tetralogy novel *The Once and Future King* about the famous castle and court of the legendary King Arthur, may also remember the implication that under his reign (King Arthur/JFK) the subjects would not have to worry about carrying an umbrella in the daytime because it would only be allowed to rain at night (Wikipedia, 2009b). This particular image packaging might have delighted the ordinary citizens, but the raingear industry would probably have been less enthusiastic.

In general, image packaging is designed to imply the candidate holds the same values as the voters. Family values are high on the list in American cultures; therefore, the candidate will be "packaged" within the circle of his family, the attractive smiling wife and a couple of healthy-looking children. If the candidate is not married yet, a supportive parent, preferably the mother, will fill the gap.

Another aspect of image packaging will place the candidate in settings that are familiar to most voters, settings that they can see themselves in. Candidates may visit factories and chat with the workers; they may be pictured at community sports events or at picnics—places where the ordinary target person feels comfortable and situations that make the target believe that the candidate is "one of us." In image marketing, positive and negative aspects are presented in a context that emphasizes the positives, so the resulting image is honest, but mainly favorable. Images are emotional; image marketing is designed to influence how people think and feel about a particular candidate.

The effects of image packaging take longer to show results than general product packaging. That's one reason to get the candidate out in the playing field long before voting time. In the manufacturing sector, image marketing is aimed at achieving a long-term brand loyalty, which is based on how the consumer feels about what is offered. Similarly, when applied to politics, the hoped-for "brand" loyalty is based on how the voter feels about what is offered by this candidate. Images remain long after the campaign has ended and whether a given candidate was victorious or not.

▦ The Use of Language

How language can be used in control attempts has already been mentioned in earlier chapters. There the focus was on language as it occurs in controlling ways in dialogues between people. In advertising and politics, language is used as a powerful tool to direct the focus of what is discussed onto a particular aspect as desired by the communicator. Because the target population can only be estimated but not definitely known by the communicator, the controlling use of language occurs along different parameters than it would in person-to-person verbal interchanges.

People do not interrogate advertising slogans when watching a commercial on TV or looking at a billboard while driving to their destination. Nobody is there to answer a question. A given product may be announced as being unsurpassed by other brands in some characteristic. Most target persons are led to believe that the other brands are not as good in that particular aspect as is the advertised brand. However, what might be true after further exploration is that the other brands, while not surpassing the advertised brand, are just as good or just as effective. The statement used in the advertising is true, but it is only a half-truth.

The choice of words in a message can be very effective in the formation of the consumer's attitude toward a given product. For instance, will consumers pick up a package of meat labeled "25% fat" more or less frequently than one labeled "75% lean?" Experimental evidence showed that consumers' attitudes were more favorable toward the "75% lean" label. Although basically the packages were identical in their proportions of fat to nonfat, the word lean made the difference because it appealed to cultural values in American customers (Pratkanis & Aronson, 2001). Image words can be used to convey a positive or negative attitude; positive image words attempt to make things sound better than they actually are or try to remove the sting from an unpleasant condition. Negative image words have the opposite effect. They make it sound as if things are much worse than they actually are.

Often words that have a positive connotation but are ambiguous in the context in which they are used make the message more appealing without disclosing the full meaning of it. Because the audience is left to make their own inferences, everybody can be happy. Richard Nixon's 1968 campaign pledge for an "honorable peace" in Vietnam found widespread acceptance. Nobody would disagree with that, but did it mean the same to everybody? Did it mean an immediate end to the war, or did the honorable peace mean unconditional surrender by the Vietnamese?

▦ The Suggestive Function of Emotional Language

Through the use of emotional language or suggestive language, communicators express approval or disapproval without giving reasons for their attitudes. Whatever the reason for a given attitude, the emotional language may influence the listener for or against an issue. Emotional language often reveals more about the speaker than about the content of the message.

Analysis of a memo with the title "Language: A Key Mechanism of Control" that was circulated by Newt Gingrich to other conservative Republicans, revealed that two sets of words were listed in the memo (Pratkanis & Aronson, 2001). The list of "optimistic positive governing" terms included expressions, such as empowering, workfare, choice, initiative, and eliminating good-time in prison. The use of those words was suggested for one's own position. In contrast, words like decay, liberal, radical, unionized, and betray were reserved for describing an opponent.

The power of words and labels to influence or control how we conceive of the world extends into many contexts besides advertising and politics. The field of social psychology includes reports of experiments that have documented the phenomenon of the self-fulfilling prophecy. The definition or description of a situation or a person can evoke behaviors that make the definition or description come true. Thus, words and labels have the power to persuade but also the power to pre-persuade, as we use them to define the reality of our social world.

The power of the mass media when employed for use in advertising or politics has already been discussed earlier in this chapter. Most would agree that television is probably the most powerful vehicle for influencing people. Television addresses our senses on different paths. There is the language; verbal messages reach our brain at the same time as our eyes observe situations and persons, but unlike photographs, the pictures come alive through the movements and actions of the people they portray. The combination is so believable that it adds up to a reflection of what could be the real world.

⬛ Controlling the Transmission of Public Information

There are various ways of silencing or stifling voices or disrupting the flow of information. On September 8, 1943, drivers in the Los Angeles Basin were forced to turn on their headlights in order to make it through the dark haze in the middle of the day. In response to this alarming news about air pollution, the *Los Angeles Times* was ready to launch an antismog campaign directed at refineries, foundries, and other smokestack industries. There was no mention about the many automobiles that might have contributed to the irritating smog. In fact, the *Times* had been extremely supportive of automobiles as agents of progress in Southern California and toward the end of 1940 had heralded the revolutionary new $5-million highway without stoplights connecting Pasadena to downtown Los Angeles, the nation's first freeway (McDougal, 2001).

In addition to having the nation's first air pollution dilemma, Los Angeles also was the first major American city experiencing traffic jams, even though the area as far back as 1902 had a public railway system. Henry Huntington's Big Red Cars offered roundtrips from Los Angeles to Long Beach, and the Pacific Electric Railway presented an extensive interurban transit system. The Big Red Pacific Electric and the yellow Los Angeles Railway formed a system of rail lines that connected hundreds of towns in Southern California. Why all these smog-producing automobiles?

After the Henry Huntington's estate had sold the two rail lines, the cars of the railways were junked and finally were replaced by slow diesel-driven buses. This transformation did not receive attention from the *Times* or other daily newspapers. Apparently, Huntington's Los Angeles Railway had been sold to American City Lines, which was a subsidiary of the National City Lines consortium. American City Lines lost no time in replacing the streetcars with buses. The list of the consortium's stockholders included such companies as General Motors, Standard Oil of California, Firestone Tire and Rubber Company, Phillips Petroleum Company, and Mack Truck.

It is not difficult to understand that each of them would benefit from a transportation system that is based in automobiles and buses. Indeed, National City Lines faced an antitrust suit in 1946, conducted in Chicago. Although the dismantling of the Los Angeles rail system was a big part of the testimony, the *Times* carried no information about that to its readers. News unfavorable to the automobile and highways were generally excluded or rationalized away in the *Times*' coverage.

This describes only one incident where the power of the media controlled the transmission of information to the public. McDougal (2001, p. 200) cites a self-published book, *Billion Dollar Blackjack*, authored by William G. Bonelli in September 1954, and describes it as "a devastating indictment of the Chandler family's greed and political power brokering throughout seven decades of the dynasty's alleged misuse of its *Times*." Those accusations are more than half a century old—are they obsolete or are they reminiscent of similar happenings today? That is anybody's guess.

▓ Tips for Control

Workshops, college courses, and books abound with recommendations and instructions for successful marketing. Recently a book on how to change minds has received public attention (Gardner, 2004). The author has observed that people spend more time trying to change other people's minds than engaging in other activities in their daily lives. When trying to influence others, most people focus on what they want without considering resistance from others. To be more effective, one needs to understand the other person's viewpoint. The list of additional tips includes suggestions such as using research and statistics to make the argument more convincing, being aware of emotional factors for special emphasis, conveying the new idea in form of a story or in pictures, approaching things from different vantage points, and being prepared to encounter small victories as well as small defeats before significant change actually happens.

There is also material available instructing salespersons and advertisers about which approach to use with a given target population, such as with women, homosexual consumers, or the "mature" consumer. Not surprisingly, women constitute the largest target population, but it goes beyond the scope of this book to present examples of techniques from the many approaches available. As a target population, women are also the most complex, because in addition to direct tactics, they can be reached through indirect approaches, such as the implied desirability by males that a given product may promise and via the persuasion of children who seemingly need certain products to become happy and well-adjusted adults.

Market researchers know that children's "disposable income" is sizable and that children also have a substantial influence on how part of the family's money is spent. In addition, marketers know that brand loyalty is established at an early age. Children want to be accepted by their peers. A boy's popularity through the image of athletic ability may be achieved through wearing a particular brand of basketball shoes. For a girl, bouncy, shiny hair, as implied by a shampoo advertisement, can be hers, and may be the path to male and female peer acceptance. When asked why they purchase particular products, children might answer that they see the product a lot or that everybody else buys it (Fox, 1996).

Compared with the general population, the group of gay consumers is rather small (about 16 percent), and the composition of profiles for use in the development of marketing tactics for reaching gays as a target population is not widespread, perhaps because it is part of the world of niche marketing, which requires different tactics. Special consideration should be given to brand names and to packaging. It is worth considering that heterosexuals may avoid particular brand products if they are aware that gays purchase them. Therefore, in order to successfully persuade consumers of both markets, it would be beneficial to create different brand names for the same product and choose different packaging styles. Considering the fact that many gays have a sizable income, their purchasing power may be an untapped reservoir for profitable marketing (DeLozier & Rodrigue, 1996).

In a book targeting the "mature market" under the heading of basic psychology more than a decade ago, readers could find suggestions on how to apply basic psychology to a sales pitch (Lewis, 1996). Demonstrating the point with the use of an example, the author compared the effects of using the standard question, "Isn't this what you want?" with the leading question, "This is what you want, isn't it?" With the second question the salesperson cleverly leads the target toward the possibility of saying yes.

Continuing with the lesson, the author explained that without the words "isn't it?" the second question would have been a command rather than a question, and senior citizens are resistive to commands. Also those words (isn't it?) make it appear that the salesperson is performing a service. Thus, the salesperson or marketer directs the customer's thoughts without being dictatorial.

Actually the author went on to explain that the salespeople *are* commanding, but their intention is to make buyers think they reached a conclusion on their own: "We're in command, and our job as professional marketers is to structure messages that work for us with maximum power" (Lewis, 1996, p. 20).

Considering the postwar baby boomers, workable approaches to motivating targets to part with their money include those that focus on exclusivity, convenience, and perhaps need for approval. The fear approach may still have power but "guilt is losing steam. 'You've earned it' washes out guilt like a stream of detergent from a hose" (Lewis, 1996, p. 149). The entitlement approach is still working well in the marketplace. Advertisements encourage prospective customers to get the vacation they deserve or the automobile they deserve—along with many other things they might deserve. No effort or expense is spared when it comes to influencing consumers in the choice of purchases and making it easy for them to part with their money in exchange for goods that they might or might not need.

This is not a book about marketing or politics. Each one of these areas could fill volumes and has already been explored by other writers. The purpose for mentioning them here is to include them as another one of the many spheres where control and power exert significant influence.

7 ▪ ▪ ▪

Control within the Self

Considerations of self-control often focus on the lack of it within an individual. For instance, in the research literature operational definitions of the absence or lack of self-control include terms like impulsivity, self-centeredness, limited concentration, quick to anger, and engaging in risky or daring activities. People with low self-control are thought to live in the here and now, and their behaviors are believed to be oriented toward immediate gratification of their desires. Furthermore, low levels of self-control are thought to be powerful predictors of physical violence and psychological aggression (Avakame, 1998). With the descriptions of its absence in mind, what are the conditions in those who seem to possess self-control?

▪ Self-Regulation

Psychologist Roy Baumeister (1997) proposed that the kind of control within the self, and which is usually thought of as self-control, would perhaps be more correctly named self-regulation. This term refers to processes that the self (the individual) applies to modify its own responses. Thoughts, emotions, and behaviors are changed in such a way that they bring about positive results. Self-regulation includes activities such as planning and goal setting, focusing attention, and overriding or inhibiting behavioral impulses. In exerting self-regulation, the individual is fully cognizant of the importance of acting and responding in ways that result in favorable outcomes for the individual. Thus, in self-regulation the target of the control attempts is the self (the individual) and the goal is to achieve something of benefit to the self or at least to avoid harm.

Even though individuals have the ability to control impulses and delay gratification in order to attain future goals, at times this ability seems to break down. In situations where the self's responses result in negative outcomes it is suspected that the self-regulation system has failed or broken down at some crucial point. Many major problems in society can be traced back to failures of self-regulatory capacity. For instance, problems with addiction, obesity, marital infidelity, and other impulsive behaviors can be understood within the framework of impaired self-regulatory functioning (Heatherton, 2000).

Development of coherent self-regulatory guidelines is largely influenced by the socializing strategies of one's parents. Individuals who have been socialized to have empathy for others and to attend to the needs of others are likely to have developed a self-regulatory style with guidelines for the self that are oriented toward others. On the other hand, individuals who were socialized by their parents to value independence and autonomy can be expected to have developed a self-regulatory style that is oriented toward their own self-guides (Moretti & Higgins, 1999).

■ Breakdown of Self-Regulation

Reasons for the breakdown of self-regulation are many and varied. Emotional distress may become so overwhelming that the individual temporarily changes the order of priorities and places termination of the distress above the application of self-enhancing responses from the self-regulatory behavior reservoir. For instance, termination of distress seems to be an important goal for some individuals who engage in cross-dressing activities. Independent of the individual's position on the continuum from transvestite to transsexual, the urge for dressing in clothes normally worn by the opposite sex is found to become more insistent at times of increased stress in the individual's life.

Peter, a successful young architect, serves as an example. Peter's wife, pregnant with their first child, had only recently found out about his secret activities. He admitted that the combined stress from meeting deadlines in his professional life, facing the new responsibilities of fatherhood, and the anxiety about his wife's reaction if she found out about his secret had caused more frequent and intense urges to cross-dress. He stated that he felt compelled to give in to these urges to reduce the level of stress he was experiencing. When asked what about his behavior brought the desired relief, he answered, "Preparing myself for passing as a woman takes such an amount of skill and deep concentration that it blocks out all my worries during that time." Peter is certainly intelligent enough to know that increased indulgence in his cross-dressing activities will most likely increase his problems, but the desire for immediate stress reduction is too overwhelming to refrain from his cross-dressing activities.

Similarly, other men who have the desire to appear as women have recognized an increase in their urges in times of high stress. As some of them explain, when they place themselves in the role and appearance of women, they feel less responsible for making decisions and for considering consequences. For a brief period they can fantasize and convince themselves that these stressful conditions have no relevance, only to return to reality with an even heavier load of stress that resulted from their excursion into fantasy.

Of course, the need for reducing stress is not the main or only reason for engaging in cross-dressing and other activities usually associated with the opposite sex. However, the fact that for the moment they are willing to engage in certain behaviors, in order to experience relief, which, in their own opinion will bring them undesirable consequences, can be understood as incidents where the self-regulatory mechanism is impaired.

In general, for most people frustration tolerance levels are significantly lower when under stress than when in calm or neutral situations. Under low frustration tolerance conditions, individuals lose the focus and concentration that are needed to consider the likely consequences of certain actions and to explore the availability of alternative responses. Drugs and alcohol provide immediate opportunities for terminating negative moods and emotions. These substances bring with them the ability to transport oneself from the stressful environment to a place of calm and relaxation. For many individuals, just the movements of pouring a drink into a glass and raising that glass to one's lips set the stage for a different mood because of the anticipated desired effects they will experience shortly.

Self-handicapping represents another category of self-defeating behavior that is under the control of the individual but produces negative outcomes. Often in order to camouflage failure, people use valid appearing excuses for not producing their best performance. Inadequate preparation for a task is a favorite and frequent excuse for protecting one's image of competence, although most people would agree that it is better to give a successful performance without excuses than to perform poorly with a good excuse. This form of handicapping reflects poor self-regulation or poor control of the self. Procrastination is a form of self-handicapping that employs logical-sounding excuses, but excuses nevertheless. At other times when procrastination is based on choosing short-term gains despite long-term costs, the individual makes the choice to indulge in immediate gratification, such as seeing a movie or spending time with friends, in favor of preparing for a task that will bring rewards later on.

Persistence, while normally a valuable strategy, can be considered self-defeating behavior when efforts persevere in the face of high-failure risks. Counterproductive persistence may be based on a (false) belief that one will eventually succeed. Setting improper or unrealistic goals constitutes yet another category of self-defeating behavior and is considered to be a consequence of disordered self-regulation. Effective goal-directed behavior then becomes a reflection of healthy psychological adaptation and adjustment as would be expected from a well-functioning self-regulatory system. Self-defeating behaviors or symptoms point toward an individual's ineffective life-course management or ineffective self-regulation.

Behavioral scientists have suggested that exploring the goals an individual originally set in comparison with the outcomes, and the individual's resulting distress symptoms, can provide an analytical pathway to the discovery of specific vulnerabilities within the ineffective self-regulation system (Karoly, 1999).

Self-management and self-regulation concepts include awareness of one's fears, which can be powerful handicapping agents within one's self-management system. In addition, there are fears that are known to others that can provide invitations for attack from other control-seeking forces in the environment. Although complete freedom from fear may appear desirable at first glance, it is unrealistic to expect it. In fact, fear can be a powerful ally in situations of real danger (de Becker, 1997).

Although people may consider the admission of fear to be a weakness, the denial of it renders the person far more vulnerable than the awareness of experiencing the fear. In the individual's awareness, the fear becomes a known entity that can be explored and worked with for options of resolution. In denial, however, fear remains an undefined, mysterious power that threatens to consume the person. One may not want to advertise the fact that one harbors certain fears, but admitting it to oneself is the first step to being able to break the fear down into manageable components. Awareness of the feared objects or situations allows for dissection into what are realistic and what might be unrealistic parts.

▓ Anger, Jealousy, and Envy: Emotions Leading to Self-Regulation Breakdowns

Mastering one's emotions is the crucial skill to achieve in the process of self-managing. Uncensored emotional responses to situations can result in high costs. In addition to disclosing one's innermost reactions to others, those emotional responses can transform a tense situation into an explosive one. Intense emotions cloud perception and reasoning and thus impair judgment. As mentioned in Chapter 3, one of the most destructive emotional reactions is anger. It distorts perception the most and is the most frequently observed reaction. Its danger lies in the seduction of feeling powerful and self-righteous. The rush from the adrenaline flow seems to have an addictive quality to it. As the individual under the influence of the intense emotion feels stronger than usual, it puts a damper on inhibitions that normally help in making reasonable decisions. Because anger is such a powerful force it is often regarded as a motivator, although the actions it motivates are usually not in the person's best interest.

Others in the environment being subjected to a person's angry eruption either respond in similar ways or withdraw. Those who withdraw for whatever reason may lead the angry person to believe that he or she has crushed the receiver into silence or retreat, which often will be interpreted as having exerted power or control over the other. For a short period of time it might even seem as if the angry person was successful in his or her moves. Thus, the good feeling from the adrenaline rush combined with the illusion of getting what one wants through exerting threatening control over others often leads to repetition of angry outbursts. Of course, every time the angry person achieves his or her goal, the explosive behavior becomes reinforced. What the angry person usually does not consider is the fact that sooner or later others will either seek revenge or leave the scene for good.

In reality, expressions of anger are not a sign of strength, just the opposite. They signal to others that the person is actually helpless, not strong or powerful enough to get what he or she wants. Individuals who have what they want have no reason to be angry; their world is treating them right. In addition to communicating the helplessness, the angry person discloses to the world what events or behaviors may ignite angry explosions and, along with that, impaired judgment. Instead of being in control, the angry person gives away control to those who are willing to push his or her emotional buttons.

Anger is not the only intense negative emotion that may have the control over others as an objective but actually leads to self-defeating behaviors: Jealousy is a complex, deeply seated emotional state that becomes part of a person's character pattern. Lazarus and Lazarus (1994) saw the personal meaning of jealousy as one of loss or threatened loss, usually the loss of love or affection from a significant other person. The individual who feels threatened with a loss will do anything within his or her power to prevent the loss or to regain what has been lost.

The scenario often includes a third party, who can be blamed for the loss and who, perhaps in addition to the love object, might serve as a target toward which to direct actions of revenge. However, vengeful actions are not always just directed at a third person. A jealous individual may threaten to or actually commit suicide in order to have the person with-holding affection punished by guilt feelings.

Jealous individuals need little provocation in order to constantly demand proof that their suspicions are groundless without ever really accepting anything as proof, short of having the desired object or person in their constant possession. In order to feel secure, having absolute control over the possession is necessary. If the target possession is a person, the goal is to have that person under constant observation or chained to an object or place from which escape is impossible.

Jealousy in common language often takes on the meaning of "envy," such as when one person exclaims to another "I am jealous of you for. . . ." followed by a description of some achievement accomplished by the other person. In general, envy is the feeling or attitude connected to a situation where the envious person wants something that another possesses. Jealousy, on the other hand, involves something that the jealous person owned but lost or is about to lose to others.

For the target person it is easy at the beginning to mistake the jealous individual's intense and ardent attention for sincere love and devotion. In fact, the intensity may resemble a passion deep enough to engulf and sweep up the target person with the jealous individual into one great fervent romance. Secretly, many of us are longing for that passionate love that will lift our experiences high above what "ordinary" loving couples feel. Novels and movies never tire of portraying couples in ecstatic embra-ces, indicating passionate romance. After paying the money for admit-tance, wouldn't the movie fan be entitled to some of those experiences too? As one client phrased it, "I want a passionate intimate relationship—is that asked too much for from life?"

What makes the attention appear so ardent and so seductive is really a passionate obsession the jealous person has with him- or herself. Viewed as a possession, the target person becomes part of the jealous individual, and the love affair is not so much a loving relationship between two indi-viduals as it is an extended self-love on the part of the jealous person. The "possession" is held onto in a gesture of fulfilling a need or as a means for self-aggrandizement.

What differentiates possessive love from healthy love is a missing ingre-dient—trust. A person consumed by obsessive love knows no trust. Jealous individuals hold a strong belief that they desperately need and are entitled to love and attention from the target person. There may also be a belief that it would be best for the target person to comply with those needs, but trust is not a part of it. Thus, to achieve what seems necessary for the controller's life, complete control over the target person is a basic requirement.

Obsessive love is not easy to recognize at the beginning of a love rela-tionship. While both people are excited about the other, they dream wonderful qualities into the other person and naturally they want to spend a lot of time together. So for a while the needs of the obsessively jealous person are met, but when the pace slows down a bit, as happens with most regular and healthy relationships, it becomes reason for concern to the jealous lover, who interprets the slow down as rejection.

Because the attention from the target person is needed as badly as air and water for the life of the jealous person, every technique is tried to hold the target captive. Sex is an often-used method; so is trying to anticipate and outguess what characteristics and qualities the target person wants in a lover. In addition to supplying and demanding sex frequently, the jealous person attempts to be the perfect companion and lover. This method is frequently observed in jealous females; the student Melanie, introduced in Chapter 4, is a good example of this approach.

Obsessive and jealous male lovers generally resort to stronger control measures, which may include emotional as well as physical restraining practices over their target persons, as discussed in Chapter 4. The only thing worse than being in a relationship with a jealous controller, is being involved with a jealous controller who has already been disappointed. Every perceived "betrayal" increases the need for control, and the target person becomes the one who is made to pay for previous rejections.

All three of these negative emotions, anger, jealousy, and envy, can give rise to various control techniques used by the afflicted individuals, but the self-defeating expression of any one of these negative emotions can render the individual's self-regulatory system impaired.

▓ Internal Struggle for Control: Obsessions, Compulsions, Superstitions

The negative emotions discussed above have a painful effect on the individual experiencing them and as we often observe, their immediate consequences seem to fall upon target persons in the individual's environment, such as a spouse or significant other with whom the individual is involved in an intimate relationship. In the case of obsessions and compulsions, however, the primary target is the self. The individual is struggling with and capitulating to the control that is exerted by the individual upon self.

Obsessions are persistent, recurring irrational thoughts, impulses, or images that a person believes he or she is unable to control. Those thoughts, impulses, or images interfere with the person's normal functioning and lead to irresistible impulses (compulsions) to perform certain behaviors in order to relieve uncomfortable negative feelings.

Lucy sincerely believed that she could not rid herself of negative thoughts without expressing them to the person who had caused them. Those thoughts would ruminate in her brain until released through action. In Lucy's case obsessive thoughts did not occur so frequently as to impair her daily functioning. The most critical area for her was concerned with her daughter Libby. Anything that looked or sounded remotely critical of Libby set her ruminations in motion, but in addition to her own discomfort, it created some socially tense moments—especially when she decided to verbalize her ruminations. Whether it concerned one of Libby's friends, or their parents, a neighbor or a teacher—if any of them treated Libby unfairly in Lucy's opinion, she could not rest until she had vented her anger. In the long run, it did not make Libby's life easier. Many of her friends withdrew from her because they did not want to encounter Lucy's tirades.

Compulsions are behavioral entities that are performed habitually and often ritually by an individual in order to achieve relief from strong negative feelings, such as anxiety, fear, or doom. The afflicted individual strongly believes that if anything should prevent him or her from performing the behavior, a catastrophe will occur. Typical compulsive behaviors include frequent hand-washing, stepping on certain spots in the pavement and avoiding others, repeated checking to see if doors are locked, or certain counting behaviors. Virtually any behavior can become a compulsion. Some people exercise compulsively, some gamble, and others may binge on chocolates or shop excessively.

While engaged in a compulsive activity, the individual gains a feeling of control and a sensation of power over the uncomfortable internal feelings of anxiety or dread. In reality, however, it is the uncomfortable feelings that create the compulsion to act with the illusion of being in control while the individual is actually out of control. The temporary feeling of power and the relief over having been distracted from the uncomfortable internal emotional turbulence are so seductive that the individual will succumb to them again and again without considering the consequences.

Lena suffered from a shopping compulsion. She had been the prettiest girl in town, when right out of high school she married the son of one of the wealthiest families in town. Her husband's family controlled her whole lifestyle. Her husband's father controlled her husband's business decisions, just as his father had dominated him in the past. For a while, at least until his father and grandfather passed away or retired, the only person left for Lena's husband to dominate was Lena. The houses that Lena and her husband lived in were chosen by her parents-in-law and also were most of the furnishings and artwork. The family maintained estates for summer and winter vacations, and the younger generations spent time there as expected. Deviations from the tradition were frowned upon. Lena's marriage was not happy, and there was much interference in how to raise her two children. Her husband took every opportunity to criticize her, and her self-esteem dwindled away.

The only area Lena was allowed to make her own decisions was in shopping for her own clothes. Everybody agreed that Lena had excellent taste.

For Lena, areas of safety were the big department stores and elegant dress shops. Here she could drown her feelings of insecurity and her unhappiness. She was in control. She held the power when she simply signed for her purchases, requesting them to be delivered to her home. Later she modeled the new clothes for herself. Sometimes she would wear one of the new outfits that evening, but mostly the clothes would disappear in the back of the closet to make room for future exciting shopping trips.

Lena's life continued like this for about three decades until their financial situation deteriorated due to some ill-advised decisions on her husband's part. Of course, he was not to blame. Because of his failing health he retired from the business and was not able to recoup what had been lost. Most of their accounts in the big stores were now closed, and Lena had to adapt to living within a rather limited budget. Her moments of control and power were reduced to driving her expensive car to the gas station or to stores and the supermarket to make needed purchases for the household. These outings did not in any way compare to the excitement of her earlier shopping sprees. Without those glorious moments Lena could no longer distract herself from the unhappiness of her life, and she sank into a deep depression, which required a long period of hospitalization.

In Lena's life, the compulsion to shop served to maintain her illusion that she was in control of her life. She became entrapped in the vicious cycle of her own creation. The illusions she created to save herself from recognizing the depth of her unhappiness and the degree to which she had been out of control burst, exposing the very lack of control she had labored so hard to keep hidden.

People's superstitions often involve certain compelling acts. The old myth that breaking a mirror opens the door for seven years of misfortune is still alive and well among us. We tend to worry and be overly cautious in our actions for a while after the mishap, but usually we stop being concerned about it long before the seven years have expired. Superstitious behaviors are similar to some of the compulsive behaviors mentioned earlier: Avoiding stepping on cracks in the pavement has the goal of avoiding encountering bad luck. There are also certain behaviors people engage in to cancel out previous behaviors that might appear to bring on misfortune. People may retrace their steps when they become aware of having stepped on cracks in pavements or stop driving or walking when a black cat has crossed their path in a certain way in front of them. As varied as the items on the list of superstitious behaviors are, they have one thing in common: They are individuals' attempts to avoid the impending doom that they believe is waiting for them in the future.

Recurring intrusive thoughts, impulsive self-defeating behaviors, and compulsive superstitious actions occur in most people's lives from time to time, and when facing reality, most of us recover from our irrational thoughts or behavioral excursions without suffering disastrous consequences. We can take the opportunity to reestablish the control in our life. When defenses to mask the fears behind the obsessive thoughts and compulsive behaviors are used excessively, to the point where they render the individual dysfunctional, the individual has been driven out of control.

▧ Exaggerated Need for Order

Bob, a tall, strong-looking man, was employed as mechanical engineer in a supervisory position at a manufacturing plant. His brown hair showed traces of gray, and his face was dominated by piercing blue eyes. During his 15-year marriage to Monica, Bob had been the undisputed head of household. Monica and their three children felt intimidated by Bob and his demands for orderliness. Although at the beginning of their marriage they enjoyed passionate lovemaking, more recently Monica had sought individual therapy for her low sexual desire, which she thought was related to Bob's tendency to criticize and control her and the children.

In Bob's opinion, there should not be a connection between the two issues because his criticism—if that's what they wanted to call it—had nothing to do with his love for his family. In fact, he did it because he loved his family and wanted the best for all of them. To Monica's surprise, Bob joined the "getting control of your life" workshop mentioned in the introduction to this book. She thought this would be the last thing Bob needed but that perhaps he wanted to obtain agreement on his opinion, which he could then report as confirmation to his family. Bob, however, did not explain his reasons.

As the group discussion turned to techniques of control that participants had observed in their interactions with others, Bob related that his wife accused him of using questions as a way of controlling her and the children. When asked for an example, Bob explained that he had found several items, a bucket, a shovel, and an empty bag, on the front porch when he came home from work. In response to his question why the items were sitting there, his wife and one of the children immediately picked up the items and disappeared into the kitchen. During dinner, the atmosphere was filled with tension; everybody ate silently. Later that night Bob tried to make love to Monica, but she was not in the mood.

Explaining the purpose of his question, Bob stated that he wanted to know who had left the items there and to make them understand that when they were finished with a task, the items should be put away in their proper storage places. Similarly to the discussion of "why" questions in Chapter 3, Bob's explanation indicated that the information about *why* was really not as important as *who* had done it. The explanation also carried the implication that the items should not be there, a fact that was not lost on the group members. "Well, I would have listened to a reasonable explanation of why the things were left out there. But, as usual, someone just forgot to put them away" was Bob's defense.

Julia, one of the female group members encountered earlier in Chapter 4, asked if these situations occurred frequently. Following Bob's confirmation that they did, she continued, "Bob, if these situations happen frequently and you act as you described it, as your wife I would feel that the main reason you come home is to criticize." She went on to say that her husband behaved in similar ways, and she felt that it did not matter whether she was there and what happened in her day. He would immediately focus on what was wrong, and that set the tone for the rest of the evening. "After that initial negative comment I don't feel like telling him that I love him."

"That's exactly what Monica says," answered Bob, "but that's wrong! Her love for me should not be involved in that. She knows that I love her and want the best for her and my family. She should support me in my attempts to take care of the family instead of accusing me of controlling everybody." Looking straight at Julia he added, "Well, don't you think we should always strive to do our best?"

"Why do I feel exactly the same as I do at home with my husband?" Julia exclaimed. At the end of their arguments—Kirk, her husband, called them "discussions"—he would say something Julia couldn't disagree with, and he would stare at her, just the way Bob did. "When I state my opinion," Julia continued, "I believe in the correctness of what I am saying. But at the end I feel forced to agree with Kirk's statements because they seem to make sense. I end up feeling totally invalidated and what is worse I don't even know how it happened"

Paul, another group member, offered his opinion, explaining that when Bob had talked about his family he was defending himself, especially to Julia. Then he ended his defense with a question of a rather general nature that nobody could disagree with—even though it was not directly related to the incidents that Bob had been talking about. Just as Julia did, Paul recognized it because it happens to him a lot. His superiors use that technique to make Paul agree with additional demands for more work. "Come to think of, my wife is using a similar approach on me when she argues for purchasing a bigger home in the country," Paul added.

The group leader explained that in this approach language was used for controlling the other person's thinking. As Paul mentioned, the question was not directly related to the incidents discussed, but it represented an irrefutable statement. The question's function was to divert the other person's attention onto a different path and forcing the other into an agreement. "Those of you who reacted to Bob's statement, what would you have liked to say to Bob? Or to your husband, to your wife, to your boss?" the leader asked.

"Stop it! You are railroading me into agreeing with you!" Julia exclaimed, still being under the impact of the verbal barrage.

If a person's line of reasoning can be predicted from previous behavior, one can prepare oneself ahead of time for the type of approach most likely used by the controller, the group leader pointed out. As Bob's final irrefutable statement was not directly related to the content of the argument, perhaps a response indicating that the person is going off on a tangent, which renders the whole discussion meaningless, might work with the added suggestion that it would be better to continue the discussion at another time.

What were Bob's goals in the interaction with his family? If he wanted things to be picked up around the house, he did get that accomplished with his questions. Was his goal to have a happy family atmosphere that evening? Apparently, that did not happen. Perhaps Bob's goal was not clearly defined in his mind, or he might have had more than one goal at the time and failed to prioritize them.

Bob's voice reflected anger as he explained his goals to be simple ones; he wants order in the house, and he wants a healthy family. The group's opinion was that these goals are not mutually exclusive and they are attainable, but that a different approach might be more successful.

At the next meeting, Bob appeared anxious to talk. "When I left here last time I felt that you were all considering me to be a control freak." Group members tried to protest but Bob told them about coming home and seeing his son standing in the kitchen with a smile on his face. As Bob's gaze went over to the kitchen table he noticed several items that were not supposed to be there. Before he could ask about those items he felt his wife tugging on his sleeve, quickly saying that Jeff wanted to tell his dad that he got an A on his math exam. Bob realized what his wife was trying to do, and he went along with it.

"Without her I would have said something about the stuff on the table and not paid attention to Jeff's good news," Bob admitted. "I still think it is important that everything is orderly and that we do our best. Perhaps I need to be attentive to other things, too. Monica was in a much better mood that evening and the atmosphere was not as tense as usual."

What would happen to his family, a group member asked, if Bob did not always comment on things that appeared a bit out of order? Would the family fall apart? Bob denied that the family would disintegrate but life would be chaotic. Bob insisted that order was important and if everybody understood that, they could be a happy family. Julia suggested that it might be an issue of focus. As Bob had admitted earlier, although he saw the smile on his son's face, his attention immediately focused on the items on the table that should not have been there. The family's focus may be related more to the moment and to pleasant events.

Bob was not about to give in: If that were the case, he insisted, the family should learn to adopt his way of focusing because it is the correct way. It works well at his job. "My people know what I expect from them, and they deliver. There is no arguing about it unless someone comes up with a better way of doing things. I will listen to what they say, but until I am convinced that their way is better, the job will be performed as was explained to them" was Bob's argument.

The group leader's suggestion that home and work environments are different in nature and therefore the relationships function on different levels, making the same approach not equally workable for every situation, did not meet with Bob's agreement. Avoiding responding to the suggestion, Bob instead addressed Paul, trying to direct the discussion to another topic, "Last time you mentioned that something I said reminded you of your boss, Paul. You would not mind explaining what you meant, would you?"

Paul, sensing something of an attack in Bob's voice, nevertheless responded as calmly as he could at the moment, clarifying that his boss, by using those irrefutable questions at the end of his stated opinion, exerts a force on the other, the target person, to agree—even though the irrefutable question may not be directly related to the topic under discussion. It is like somebody took away the target person's freedom to behave in ways opposite to the person who made the statement, and, of course, that is the plan behind it!

Continuing with the line of discussion, the leader explained that by ending a discussion or argument with a statement nobody can disagree with, an air of righteousness is lent to the whole argument. It makes it appear as if the speaker is correct, even though that is not necessarily the case. However, just because the person placed these question statements at the end of his opinion did not mean that the other person has to respond to them. One can respond to any part that one wants to address. In fact, psychologists have suggested that people observe the difference between content and process in verbalizations. Those irrefutable statements or questions are not part of the content; they are actually representing a process, the process of controlling the listener's response.

Controlling behavior is not one-directional; it occurs in both directions—from the controlling person to the target and from the target person in some ways back to the controller. Some of the target person's own behaviors may actually invite, encourage, or empower the controlling person to apply his or her strategy. Controlling behaviors do not occur in a vacuum nor do they happen without a reason. Often there is a common element between the controlling person and the target person, and this element is fear. It seemed that Bob controlled his family out of the fear that there would be chaos if he did not observe and criticize. His family members did not openly rebel, perhaps out of fear that he would not provide as well for them.

As Bob had mentioned, the family atmosphere had been more pleasant when he refrained from immediate criticism. If Bob valued the friendlier atmosphere as something of benefit to him, he probably could think of alternate ways to communicate his preference for orderliness in the house, such as praising when the rooms look neat.

"Funny you would say that; I have thought about giving that a try," Bob admitted with some hesitation in his voice, "although I still believe that correct behaviors should occur automatically without any need for praise." Bob's statement demonstrated that acting in self-controlling ways is more difficult to achieve than controlling others.

■ Self-Management Activities

Goal setting, planning, and decision making are multiple acts of self-regulation that have been grouped together under the term self-management. These important forms of self-management can aid people in their attempts to regulate themselves effectively and successfully or they can backfire and undermine one's efforts (Baumeister, Heatherton, & Tice, 1994). All too often, self-defeating behaviors appear avoidable and therefore especially sad because they "are perpetrated by people who are indeed generally striving for positive outcomes, but who bring misfortune or failure on themselves" (Baumeister, 1997, p. 168).

Techniques learned as a Navy SEAL for overcoming inherent weaknesses and implementing the power of self-discipline offer effective guidelines for the improvement of self-management (Janke, 2000). According to this system, the beginning of self-discipline lies in accepting that individuals have control over their thoughts, actions, and words and they can learn to control them with self-discipline. Setting well-defined goals and planning the individual steps necessary to achieve those goals are the first stepping-stones on the path to self-mastery. Avoidance of procrastination and swift implementation of action plans will transform individual steps into elements of reality. Reviewing progress, and where necessary modifying plans to ensure successes along the chosen path, can be used as safeguards for achieving specified goals. Self-mastery, or control over self, requires the individual's efforts at every point along the continuous process.

However, on the encouraging side, Navy SEAL Michael Janke explained that if an individual can do anything for a period of 14 days, that person has already started to develop a life-changing habit. Continuing persistently with the changed behavior will turn it into a powerful part of the person's overall lifestyle (2000, p. 103): "Persistence is what separates the successful people from the almost-successful people."

■ Self-Managing Charisma

More than 20 years ago social psychologist Ronald Riggio (1987) described John Fitzgerald Kennedy as an example of a "Charisma Profile"—a study that is still of interest. According to Riggio, Kennedy's greatest strength was his extraordinary emotional control. Insisting on distancing himself from displays of emotion, his personality appeared to be in complete control. Where a certain degree of emotional expression and sensitivity contribute to the charisma of some leaders (Martin Luther King Jr. and Robert F. Kennedy), the restriction and containment of his own emotions added to John F. Kennedy's charisma by giving him the appearance of being objective and analytical, and also of being a sensitive and interested listener, considerate to the emotional concerns of others. A high degree of self-control is required of the charismatic leader who ". . . engages in impression management—carefully controlling outward appearance—to cover up any personal weaknesses in an effort to continue receiving the group's respect, admiration, and support" (Riggio, 1987, p. 83).

Reportedly, as a young man, John F. Kennedy was fascinated by the attraction and magnetism that movie stars seemed to possess. While visiting Hollywood he was determined to meet and observe such stars as Clark Gable, Gary Cooper, and others (Riggio, 1987). Observing the behavior of others and noting desirable or successful consequences coming to the observed person, can provide valuable roadmaps for those who want to improve their own effectiveness. These observations are congruent with psychologist Albert Bandura's formulations of social cognitive theory discussed in Chapter 6.

■ Self-Help Books and Self-Control

Not everybody has the time or resources to travel to Hollywood and watch successful movie stars. Self-help books may be the answer for those who have to study at home. There was a time when books on assertiveness sprang onto the market like daffodils after a spring rain. The sheer number of available books on that topic would make us believe that after reading them there would not be a single unassertive person left in this world. In fact, most people's behaviors have not changed much despite the seemingly limitless supplies of advice offered by the American publishing industry and bookstores, ranging from improving relationships to handling just about every imaginable crisis.

Sometimes people intent on improving themselves or their relationships, bring self-help books to their therapists to discuss the desired changes. One therapist remembered when several years ago a female client brought the book *Women Who Love Too Much* (Norwood, 1985) into the session, handing it to the therapist. The paperback book's weight was enhanced by 57 paperclips, which marked the pages the client wanted the therapist to pay special attention to while reading the book. This situation may reflect the client's eagerness for change, but it also constitutes an attempt to control the therapist's reading choices.

This is not to say that self-help books are not of value, and at times therapists may suggest specific books to their clients in order to facilitate certain aspects of self-management. Many of the books are excellent in describing the problem but may not always include recommendations on how to be different. Others have step-by-step directions on how to change behavior, but there is nothing to keep the reader from putting the book aside without applying the directions or instructions consistently. Therapists are aware that after some early attempts at behavior change the book may be left on the shelf to collect dust. If therapists become involved with their clients' reading materials, should they remind clients to return to the reading or should they respects their clients' rights to enter other avenues for learning and practicing self-management? The choice lies with the individual therapist's beliefs.

▦ Self-Regulatory System Repair

The group members' reactions gave Bob a wake-up call about his expectations of his family's actions and his behaviors when his expectations were not fulfilled. He had felt an emotional isolation from his wife and children, which disturbed him, but he had difficulties abandoning his firm belief that he was doing the best for his family when he insisted on order in the house. During his group participation he learned to recognize that his manner of operating at his workplace did not bring satisfying results when applied at home.

Bob considered himself a disciplined person but was unaware of the fact that the power of self-discipline included planning, goal-setting, and decision making as well as reviewing his progress and modifying his plans when necessary in order to achieve specified goals. Change was difficult for Bob; once his goals had been set and his plans were defined, he was reluctant to reconsider any part of it. This was the area where his self-regulation system was weakest.

Because he concentrated on his goal of order in the house, he lost sight of another goal—to enjoy a warm and intimate relationship with Monica, his wife. The love and respect he expected from his children was intertwined with fear, prohibiting the development of close parent-child interactions. It was time for defining goals accurately and establishing safeguards for reaching those goals, along with implementing impression-management skills for achieving the appearance of being an objective but caring person, considerate of his family members' emotional concerns. Repairing failures in one's regulatory system requires a high degree of self-control and self-discipline.

■ Self-Discipline from Beginning to End

Self-discipline, as previously mentioned, was seen by Janke (2000) as a power that can be achieved through learning to control one's thoughts, beliefs, and actions. Self-discipline is also considered an important ingredient in the pursuit of Greene and Elffers's (1998) 29th law of power, which states, "Plan all the way to the end." All possible consequences, obstacles, and shifts of fortune need to be considered in the planning of a strategy. Of equal importance is the knowledge when to stop, as pointed out by Machiavelli long ago, "Wise princes and republics should content themselves with victory; for when they aim at more, they generally lose. . . . [W]hen this false hope [of more than victory] takes possession of the mind, it makes men go beyond the mark, and causes them often to sacrifice a certain good for an uncertain better" (Machiavelli, 1950, p. 375).

History can provide some lessons on that. The Prussian premier Otto von Bismarck believed that Prussia was fated to become a significant power on the European map. His first move was to start a war with Denmark to recover former Prussian territories. Knowing that France and England would worry about his move, he enlisted Austria in the war. Then in 1866 Bismarck influenced the Prussian king to withdraw from the German Federation, which had been dominated by Austria, and to face Austria in a war. The powerful Prussian army defeated the Austrians within seven weeks. Although the king and the Prussian generals wanted to take Austrian lands, Bismarck stopped this, placing himself on the side of peace and negotiating a treaty with Austria that would establish Prussia as the dominant power in Germany with leadership of the newly formed North German Federation. Europe was afraid of Bismarck's next move, but he did not initiate any new wars. He founded the German Empire with the Prussian king as crowned emperor.

What people did not know was that Bismarck's goals had been Germany's security and independence, not the increase of the German territory, as the other European countries feared. Once he had achieved his goal he stopped. He never let triumph go to his head; he was not tempted by the siren call of more. "Whenever the generals, or the king, or the Prussian people demanded new conquests, he held them back. Nothing would spoil the beauty of his creation, certainly not a false euphoria that pushed those around him to attempt to go past the end that he had so carefully planned" (Greene & Elffers, 1998, p. 241). He was not tempted by the possibility of further riches and glory. When his goal was reached, "[H]e withdrew into his shell like a turtle. This kind of self-control is godlike" (p. 243).

Drawing the parallel to the lives of individuals, a person in the limelight might get away with being engaged in an extramarital affair with one secret lover, but may ask for trouble flaunting a whole harem in the face of the spouse and the public. In addition, as indicated by the example of Bismarck's actions, the effects of self-control are further enhanced by silence. Instead of explaining our actions to those around us, silence surrounds our actions with mystery. It is tempting to have our vanity gratified by reaping applause for our hard work or cleverness. Yet if we are able to perform our tasks without complaints and with apparent ease, people will be in awe. If those around us believe the task was an easy one for us to accomplish, they will think that we are endowed with special talents or greater powers than they are.

8 ▪ ▪ ▪

Re-Creating One's Self

Returning to Janke's (2000) notion of self-mastery or control over self, as discussed in the previous chapter, the most significant impact of a person's control over self can be observed in instances where the person re-creates the self and is making conscious decisions to forge a new persona or identity instead of accepting the roles that society has enforced on that person. Such an undertaking requires enormous efforts. There are decisions to be made regarding which characteristics to include in the new identity. Planning how to attain and reflect the new characteristics, observing consequences of new behaviors, rehearsing and practicing, and modifying and fine-tuning desired behaviors are all necessary steps in the process. Above all, making certain that new behaviors are congruent with underlying values and beliefs is a prerequisite for achieving success.

Many people believe that their personality is fixed at birth or early in their lives, while others realize that their parents and other significant people in their environment have shaped many of their character traits. Some agree with Plato (1991, p. 425-B; original publication 1968): "The direction in which education starts a man will determine his future life"; others may argue, "Why should I be saddled with traits that don't work for me?" They may refuse to allow others the control over what their personality should be like. Instead, they assume the responsibility for forming their own identity according to their preferences. The process of self-creation, of sculpting one's persona might seem like an overwhelming undertaking, but it can also be understood as having the freedom to make one's own choices.

Although it may sound revolutionary, the idea of re-creating oneself is by no means a new one. In about 545 BCE Theogenis is said to have made the suggestion "Adopt the character of the twisting octopus, which takes on the appearance of the nearby rock. Now follow in this direction, now turn a different hue" (quoted in Beck, 1968, 77; from *Elegies*, p. 215).

In the 19th century, a young woman who wanted to be a writer was told by an editor that she would be better off making babies and not literature. Women writers were regarded as second-rate artists and mainly were expected to write for female readers. In response to the editor's rejection of her work, the young woman decided to re-create her public image and play the part of a man. She dressed in men's clothes and smoked cigars, drank, and conversed with men. She assumed the power to determine her own character, controlling the image to be presented to the public and controlling the part that remained private. Her first major novel was published under the pseudonym George Sand, and George Sand remained her public persona.

In the late 20th century, another woman commanded the world's interest through manipulation of the images she presented to the public. Madonna Ciccone became a visual symbol, invented and reinvented by herself. She used her arsenal of images to do battle with conventional prescriptions that limit her identity in particular and female identity in general. "Madonna *works* that psycho-visual runway: she is mannish, she is girlish, she is virginal, she is whorish, she is Marilyn Monroe, she is James Dean; she is Aphrodite, she is Dionysus, she is whoever she chooses to be; . . . And although one way of explaining the ease with which Madonna unabashedly shifts the presentation of her persona is to call it 'taking control' (and this has been the standard media interpretation), another way is to say that these shifts represent a kind of fearlessness" (Turner, 1993, pp. 11–12).

Rather than let others define her image for her, Madonna took control to be the master of her own image, one that has had no boundaries assigned to it by anyone. In addition, she apparently realized that any one of her "characters" could grow stale over time. By dramatically altering and reinventing her characters, she avoided the public's ability to predict her behaviors.

It is interesting to note that we measure the talent and value of an actor or actress by the diversity of roles or characters they can represent believably. Why should it be surprising to see that "ordinary" people might want to re-create their identities? Greene and Elffers (1998, p. 191) suggest: "Do not accept the roles that society foists on you. Re-create your-self by forging a new identity, one that commands attention and never bores the audience. Be the master of your own image rather than letting others define it for you. Incorporate dramatic devices into your public ges-tures and actions—your power will be enhanced and your character will seem larger than life."

Restructuring one's personality can be a lifelong process as experiences from one's past and present interactions and relationships with others intertwine with one's internal and external reactions to those experiences. Psychologists who ascribe to the constructionist view consider the self as a lifelong organizing process that represents patterns of affect, which include construction, action, and other experiential aspects. All experience is thought to arise from the realm of the self, which determines its possi-bilities and limitations.

Psychologists who adhere to the rationalist view, on the other hand, emphasize the control of self by means of ritualized techniques. In the constructivist view, intense emotions are considered to be expressions of people's past and future development, which can serve as powerful allies. In the rationalist approach intense emotions are regarded as undesirable emotions that lead to the development of individuals' problems (Mahoney, 1991). Thus, personality restructuring can occur along different paths, depending which view one adheres to.

▥ Taking Control of Your Life Workshop—An Arena for Self-Restructuring

Ongoing workshops like the one mentioned in the introduction and in the previous chapter serve as an arena for exploration, planning, and practice for participants tackling issues of control and manipulation in their lives. Becoming aware of one's involvement in control schemes with their many facets and understanding their dynamics are just the initial steps. How to use control wisely and how to protect oneself from the damaging effects of others' harmful control attempts require additional efforts and learn-ing. Such learning can best be achieved in a workshop setting with others who have similar goals. Participants in such a setting, while focusing on solutions for their own situation, have additional opportunities to learn vicariously from the efforts of their fellow participants. In addition, a group experience as provided in such workshops presents opportunities for applying new insights and practicing new behaviors within a protected environment.

Julia, one of the workshop participants, who was mentioned in Chapter 4 and in the previous chapter, had a history of marrying intelligent but controlling men. She described her difficulties with asserting herself in her marriage to Kirk: "Over the years we have had some arguments over expenditures. We are quite different in our outlook on finances. Kirk makes big purchases and wants to buy the best, whereas I am rather frugal. I don't like to go into debt."

Julia continued to explain how last year they were considering the purchase of a new car. Kirk suggested an outrageously expensive car, which Julia immediately rejected. About a week later Kirk suggested another automobile. Julia still thought it was too expensive for their budget. However, Kirk outlined all the safety features of the car, ending with, "You would want to have the safest car possible for our children, wouldn't you? You already turned down the other car which was even better on safety features than this one." Against her better judgment they bought the second car, even though it represented a financial hardship.

The other day Kirk had talked about needing a new TV and provided printed materials on a TV set with all kinds of sophisticated features, a home entertainment system. Of course, the price was high and Julia rejected it right away. Then she remembered the car situation and was curious to see if Kirk would try the same approach again. A few days elapsed before his second attempt. Just like before, he presented information about another TV set, somewhat lower in price but still too high for Julia's taste. When she hesitated, he summarized again all the great features, ending with, "You would want our children to be able to watch the Discovery Channel and learn from other valuable programs, wouldn't you?" After all, this was already a compromise to the TV he had originally suggested. Before he could continue with his argument, Julia calmly stated that the children were perfectly able to watch those valuable programs on their current TV.

Another group member asked how Kirk had responded to Julia's refusal to purchase the expensive TV. According to Julia, he was upset and tried to continue the argument the following day, but she did not change her mind. "What really kept me from caving in was that I recognized he was using control techniques on me, which he had successfully applied for years without my being aware of it." Now she could see what his goals were, and as the target she could even predict his techniques! She admitted that it saddened her to realize that he was using those control attempts on her and that the techniques he used were designed to convince her that he respected her opinion, when they were really meant to get him what he wanted. With this method they were already in debt to a dangerous degree. Now that her eyes were opened, she might have to reevaluate her marriage and her trust in Kirk.

Although everyone wanted to cheer for her, Julia's last remark left a note of sadness. The leader confirmed that it was disappointing for Julia to observe her husband's manipulation. Apparently, Kirk was using a well-known persuasion technique, commonly called the door-in-the-face technique, where the controller starts with a rather large request, which he knows will probably be denied but then follows up with a smaller request that he hopes the target person will accept because it is smaller and because of feeling guilty over the previous rejection. Julia's discovery of Kirk's control tactics could influence the trust and good feelings in her marriage, the leader agreed, but it would also increase the trust in her own ability to recognize control schemes that were directed at her.

Looking at the leader, Julia said, "Some time ago you made a statement about people building meaningful lives for themselves; it kept coming back to me and I wondered what would be my focus of interest as well as income if my marriage does not improve as I am hoping and my children are grown and have moved away? With just a four-year college degree in liberal arts, what could I do now or in 10 years?"

Julia continued to tell the group how recently she had become friendly with a neighbor who is an attorney and works mostly from home now while her children are young. Julia enjoyed listening to her neighbor talk about her work and mentioned that she was searching for something that could lead to a possible career. The neighbor suggested Julia might check out training to become a paralegal.

Last week, Julia followed up on that and attended a career seminar at a local university. She obtained information about different programs and was pleased to learn that she could enroll in a paralegal certificate program. Her children were still young, and she would have to proceed slowly with the classes; however, apparently, there were provisions for people who needed to attend on a part-time basis.

Julia admitted that she would like to enroll in the program, ". . . but there is the issue of tuition. I doubt that my husband will be happy to spend that kind of money on me," she explained. "Kirk is always talking about saving college money for the kids and then for our retirement, even though that is unrealistic, given our current financial situation. That's when I decided to carefully introduce the idea to him by focusing on the income I could earn even before the children are ready to leave for college. If we invest in this now, there will be many years I can earn money for the family."

"So you are trying to control your husband," Bob pointed out. "Just as he is controlling me," Julia responded somewhat defensively, "but as I had almost expected, he said that I could probably earn money doing something else when the time comes. However, he did not say no. I am trying to make it easier for him to help me earn money for the family." Reminding the participants of an earlier session she continued, "Control is not a one-way street, as we learned earlier in this workshop. Everybody is controlling in some way or another."

With a smile, Bob added, "I guess, I have just provided another practice opportunity." Pointing to herself, Julia continued in a soft voice, "I have let it happen to me long enough. All these years, I have let my husband make the decisions, or I quietly accepted it when he decided on something without consulting me. I did not realize that I have invited him or empowered him to control my life and my future. It took this workshop to open my eyes, and it would be foolish not to apply what I have learned so far. I am not blaming my husband; I am finally accepting the responsibility for my own wishes. Although I hope that in the end my whole family will benefit, it is also something I want to do for myself."

"What are you going to do about it? Discuss it again with your husband," Wilma, another group member inquired.

"I am not bringing it up again," Julia answered. "Perhaps you can call it manipulating, but I went ahead and proceeded with the general enrollment. I'll start with one course, an introductory course, and go from there."

Wilma agreed that it is sad that women sometimes can't afford to disclose the whole truth. When it comes to their own interests, they need to be diplomatic. At least, Julia's husband did not say "no" to her plans when she first told him about it. Laughingly she added, "Why give him a second chance to say no?"

Julia mentioned that she had another opportunity to talk to her neighbor and got some guidelines on what a paralegal gets paid but, more importantly, she offered to pay Julia if she would type her briefs for her. Because the neighbor works a lot from her home now, she makes notes and dictates, and even though their typists at the law office would do her typing, she thought it would be worth her while to have someone near her home to check out things or to do it on short notice. She is willing to pay for the convenience, and Julia could make a bit of money while becoming familiar with the legal language.

Wilma added in an excited voice, "Who knows, if you work well with your neighbor, there might even be a job waiting for you at the neighbor's law practice when you have completed your studies."

Julia seemed happy; having received encouragement and well-meaning attention for her plans was a new experience for her. Then turning to Bob, she inquired about his family, as he had not said much lately.

Bob answered, "We are working on some changes. I still don't like it when things are out of order, but I have asked Monica to help me become aware of special occasions as she did when my son got an A on his math exam. Monica gently pointed out that criticism on those occasions, even when they have nothing to do with the special event, dampen or undermine—her word—motivation. Actually, I think she is trying to train me. I noticed that I am holding back with criticism until I have seen her, just to make sure that I am upholding my end of the bargain. Monica is a smart woman."

"It sounds like you are admiring her," was Julia's response. "You are right," Bob agreed. "I admire her rather than blaming her for controlling me—isn't that what you meant?" Julia laughed, nodding her head.

Obviously, participants have already incorporated into their lives parts of what they learned, either by direct action or by planning for action, the leader pointed out. For some of their plans action might take a while. "We are not dealing with black and white situations where someone tries to control you and you just simply assert yourself. Recognizing what is happening and responding appropriately to different situations is much more complicated but ultimately rewarding in the end."

▓ Me and My Shadow—An Example of Self-Restructuring

Jonathan, the shy young man, introduced in Chapter 5, realized the need for change, but he experienced difficulty in actually doing it. It was painfully clear to him that he might never gain his father's approval. In addition, Jonathan was still suffering over the breakup with Susie. He regarded himself as a complete failure; there was no area in his life where he saw himself as succeeding.

For about two years, Jonathan had been dating Susie, a pretty young woman with a ready smile and a twinkle in her bright blue eyes. Socially, Susie was everything Jonathan was not. He was enchanted by her outgoing personality. Even his father approved of her—hesitatingly. Susie recognized the impact that his father's control had on Jonathan, and she encouraged him to start asserting himself. She had hoped that he would build a life of his own, one that he could share with her. When Jonathan's father invited Annette's husband to join the family business, Susie warned him that his time to take a more assertive stand would soon run out. Jonathan did not act on her advice; he continued to hope that by pleasing his father he could achieve his father's acceptance of him. Susie terminated the relationship knowing that Jonathan had decided against his own best interests. While he tried to avoid his father's rejection, Jonathan lost Susie's acceptance and support.

Now that once again his father had made important business decisions without discussing any aspect of them with Jonathan, the time had finally come for Jonathan's participation in the "taking control of your life" workshop.

At the first meeting of the ongoing workshop, participants introduced themselves, some hesitatingly, others somewhat more confident. After stating his name Jonathan added, "I hope this workshop will help me become more assertive; I've even flunked self-help books." One of the female participants nodded her head in agreement, mentioning that she, too, had tried that approach without success. Most of the workshop enrollees stated as their goals learning to defend themselves and to get out from under the control exerted over them by others. Bob briefly stated that his wife had accused him of being controlling.

The group leader asked participants to relate situations in which they felt having been controlled by someone else. Participants brought up scenarios like "if you feel uneasy or find yourself having done something you didn't want to do" or "when you realize that you did not get to do what you had intended to do." The leader agreed that those were situations where one could identify oneself as the target of control attempts. Although in some cases the controller's intentions might remain hidden for a while, usually it was not difficult to pinpoint the source of the manipulative action, the controller.

"So, you know that you have been the victim or target—what do you do then?" asked Julia, the young woman who earlier had agreed with Jonathan regarding the use of self-help books.

"At the time you realize that you are or have been the target, you have choices," the leader answered. "You can become angry and waste time and energy on planning revenge, or you can study the controller's method and estimate the intended goal, unless this was a one-time encounter. If you know that you will never meet the person again, you may not want to bother with it."

"What do you do when the controlling person is part of your everyday life?" Julia asked again.

"Then you can expect that similar behaviors from the controller will come your way again," responded the leader. "With observation and studying, the target person can prepare and take precautions to avoid becoming the victim again. Most controlling persons have a limited repertoire of techniques and use them repeatedly. They don't spend the time and effort to reinvent the wheel but most likely resort to the techniques that have been successful in the past."

As a homework assignment, the leader gave each participant a "control worksheet" to complete. The worksheet requested a brief description of an event during which the participant felt controlled by others. The description should include clear definitions of the originator and the target (usually the self) of the particular event, as well as a brief estimate of the originator's goal. In addition to noting the group member's feelings and responses at the time of the event, the participants were asked to identify how, in retrospect, they would have wanted to feel and respond in the described situation.

Completion of the worksheet places participants right at the core for working on desired changes. It also introduces the opportunity to influence the consequences of the originator's future control attempts. The request for information about how they would have wanted to respond establishes the notion that they are not helpless and that there are alternative options. Individuals can choose to remain willing victims, or they can decide to free themselves from the controlling influences of others.

As group members entered the room at the next meeting, they gravitated toward the same seats they had occupied in the previous session. The leader pointed out how people tend to feel comfortable in the same placements and how it helps in remembering each group member's name. Jonathan, who had been quiet during the previous meeting, related the situation to his own life, telling the group how it reminded him of his father's house. His father insisted that the whole family show up for dinner every Friday evening. "We usually sit in the same chairs; but, of course, we don't sit down before he and my mother have taken their seats" he continued. "There is very little change. My father strongly believes in consistency of behavior and action. In his opinion, consistency gives a person an aura of dignity and stability."

The group members seemed interested in hearing more about the family dinners and Jonathan continued, "At the dinner, nobody would dare take a bite before my father has given the signal. The conversation usually revolves around the business and everybody's family obligations. There is very little laughter because we have to be careful about what we say. My father is very critical and easily offended, although at the time he may not express that verbally; instead he keeps a running log in his head of what he terms unacceptable behaviors."

Could one skip one of the meetings, a group member asked. Jonathan explained that this would amount to an unpardonable sin, for which there would be no forgiveness. He knows because he had committed that sin a couple of months ago when he performed his comedy act at the club. Jonathan's father used his long-established system of punishment. Whenever someone is not at the Friday dinner he discusses some important plans or events that will affect the absent family member and the unspoken rule is that no one else informs that family member.

"After having committed the unpardonable sin, I see no options for myself to gain a secure base within the family. I have no resources. I am totally dependent on my father, and he has always disapproved of what I wanted to do."

Picking up on the hopelessness in Jonathan's voice, the leader suggested that before the situation was declared hopeless, they should examine what was known: The father's goal appeared to be the absolute control over the business and the family. His control techniques, as described by Jonathan, included providing limited information, using silence with threatening undertones, and his reluctance to ask questions. His target was probably the whole family, but at the moment, Jonathan might be the special target. What can be assumed about the consequences of the father's applied control techniques?

"Everybody is scared of him and does what he wants," Julia said, "and he has it set up so that everybody competes with everybody, which makes everybody else weaker than he is," echoed Paul, another group member.

These were excellent observations, the leader agreed; what could Jonathan do to change the situation? Suggestions ranged from quitting his job and working for someone else to telling his father that he was splitting up the family, which was a bad thing to do.

"Thanks for coming up with suggestions," Jonathan replied but then explained that talking to his father would actually make his situation worse. He needed the paycheck, as small as it was. Another job? Aside from wanting to be a comedian, the furniture business was all he knew, and he didn't know enough of it to work for another store. They were doing business the old-fashioned way, not using computers to show customers how the furniture would look in the customer's house by using room and furniture measurements as well as colors and manipulating them on the computer. Even their bookkeeping system was not fully computerized. Besides, he could not join the competition against his own family.

Agreeing that talking to his father would not be beneficial, the leader pointed out that the situation might appear more hopeless than it really was. The father's use of rituals and silence as tools in his control system gave Jonathan the advantage of being able to predict his father's behavior. As stated in *The 48 Laws of Power* (Greene & Elffers, 1998), a person's predictability is understood as giving others an opportunity for control. Humans are creatures of habit, and most people have a feeling of comfort within a predictable environment; changes reduce this comfort. In fact, unpredictability can be used to keep others in a state of suspended terror.

Jonathan wanted to know how predicting his father's silence could help because he didn't know what his father was thinking and what he would do.

The leader responded by explaining that while Jonathan did not know his father's thoughts, he could use his energy to plan and work on what would be in his own best interest, independent of his father's thoughts and actions. He could quietly work on educating and equipping himself with skills that would modernize the operations of the furniture business, so that he would be ready when it was needed. Improving his marketable skills would not only be in Jonathan's favor for assuming more responsibility for the store when the time came, it also would be of benefit in case he needed to seek employment elsewhere. With the knowledge of the father's ritual in presiding over the dinner conversation, Jonathan could predict when he was expected to speak up and when to remain quiet. Of course, this approach would not bring the satisfaction of immediate improvement.

However, Jonathan could make another one of his father's control techniques work in his favor, too. The father's tendency not to ask questions would protect Jonathan from having to disclose his plans. The fact that his father, similar to other people, likes to be consistent in his behaviors because of his belief that it reflects a certain degree of dignity would further aid Jonathan in keeping his plans secret. As long as Jonathan showed up for the Friday dinners, discussed a few business matters but remained silent about his own plans and activities, he could change the consequences of his father's control approaches to his advantage. Jonathan could decide to be an observer, not just a forced participant, and he could learn from his observations.

"Target persons become victims when they accept the controller's unacceptable behaviors," the leader continued. "In the scenario that group member Bob had described in an earlier meeting, his wife seemed to feel that Bob was either criticizing or controlling the family's behavior with his questions. Similarly, Julia had been the target of her husband's criticism for some time before considering change. Jonathan's family accepted the father's tendency to *not* ask questions as a control measure that made them think the father knew everything already, and with that he also implied that others in the family should not ask or communicate because he regarded that as gossiping. It worked because the family members went along with this, apparently for several years and for various reasons of their own. Could they have changed their opinion about it now and decided it was important for them to communicate?"

The leader went on to point out that when Jonathan accepted his father's behaviors without doing anything to protect himself, he enabled his father to continue with his controlling behaviors without any disturbing consequences to himself. If Jonathan realized that he was not helpless, that he had some means of control, at least over what he did, he could shift the impact of the consequences in his favor. By giving his father's refusal to ask questions a new interpretation—meaning that he did not have to inform his father about his activities (quite the opposite from his past attitudes when Jonathan hoped that being open and disclosing his ideas would bring him his father's acceptance), he would now protect himself instead of rendering himself vulnerable. Jonathan could utilize his father's behavior in a new, self-enhancing way.

At the next meeting, Jonathan arrived early. The group leader inquired about Jonathan's plans regarding the issues discussed in the previous meeting. Jonathan's response indicated that he had decided to proceed slowly. He had collected information about computer classes to improve his marketability. Also, he thought he could make a few changes regarding his position in the family and at work. At the family dinners, he planned to make a suggestion about the business from time to time without insisting that it be adopted. He would also gradually increase his visibility in the store. Because of his low self-confidence he had stayed in the back, which was what his father apparently wanted. "However, I realize that it would be better for me if customers associated me with the store. My natural inclination has been to hide in the back—or behind a comedy routine when I had the ambition to become a comedian."

"Let's look at your use of words for a moment," the leader said, pointing out that Jonathan had called it his natural inclination to hide in the back while he also thought that his father *wanted* him in the back of the store. "Perhaps what you called a 'natural inclination' is not so natural after all." The leader went on to note that Jonathan's father seemed to take a rather authoritarian, if not dictatorial, stance. Individuals like that usually assume a position of importance and tend to push others into the background. In other words, the father did not exactly go out of his way to make his son feel special; so what Jonathan called natural might well have been a notion that his father had induced in him. "Had your father instilled more self-confidence in you as you were growing up, you might not have thought of hiding yourself. Rather than accepting hiding as your natural tendency, you can look at it as having been imposed upon you when you were vulnerable because of your young age and limited capacity for judgment. Your decision to proceed slowly will serve you well. I just wanted to direct your attention to a factor that may make your transition more logical and easier."

In the meantime, other group members had arrived and entered the discussion. They wanted to know how one would ever know what is natural or inborn and what has been imposed upon us by others. The leader suggested, "You could start by acting in ways that do not seem 'natural' to you or what you might call your temperament or your personality style. And it would be good not to quit after a few times because in the beginning, new behaviors make us feel awkward, which could easily lead us to quit. After a while, the different behaviors may feel more comfortable and may help us in accomplishing what we want. If acting in new ways continues to result in great discomfort, we can always discontinue, but we have given ourselves a chance to explore if we could do things differently."

Bob disagreed: "It sounds like you are throwing the whole concept of personality wide open. I learned in a psychology class that our personality is formed in childhood."

The foundations for our personality are laid in childhood, the leader agreed, but as stated before, our capabilities to make appropriate judgments are not well developed in early childhood—and a lot of what we accept for truth is often what we have been told from those around us: parents, teachers, or religious leaders. "Wouldn't you want to have input into what constitutes something so important as your character or personality?" The question was meant as a stimulus to give this idea more serious consideration.

Continuing with the discussion, the leader pointed out that the notions of the significance of early childhood influences and the possibility of later modification by the individual are not mutually exclusive. There is no doubt that how a child is raised is extremely important for its later development. Our behavior patterns reflect that fact, but individuals do have opportunities to explore how to modify those aspects that are not of benefit to them. For instance, a person who has a strong tendency to frequently act out of anger may find it difficult to have friends or others who would help him or her if help were needed. For that person it would be advantageous to change or modify some of the behaviors and their underlying reasons.

Of course, strongly held beliefs that change is impossible will prompt individuals not to even try; it wouldn't make sense attempting to do something that we are convinced is impossible to do. Strongly held beliefs can give direction and guidance to our lives; however, when not examined or challenged, strong beliefs can also keep doors to new opportunities closed.

"According to what you said, my father may have manipulated me to behave in ways that I believe are part of my natural disposition and by continuing to behave in the same way, I am unknowingly continuing with my father's manipulation of me." Jonathan summarized his understanding of the leader's statements.

"That's one way of looking at it. Understanding the situation in that light provides another option, the option to be different," the leader agreed.

"When parents don't listen to us or don't pay much attention to us, are they manipulating us into thinking we are not worth much?" asked Betty, another female group member.

Manipulating might be too strong a word suggested the leader. Many parents attempt to control their children's future because they really want the best for them and they are convinced that they have the knowledge and wisdom to do so. With their own behaviors, they shape their children's actions. They indicate to their children how the children are expected to act. There is no doubt that parents have control over their children to varying degrees; some use that control with the best intentions for their children, whereas others might have ulterior motives at heart. Disregarding the reason for the moment, not being listened to or not given attention could easily instill in a child the belief that he or she is not worth the attention and could in turn lead to the development of poor self-esteem in that person.

At the beginning of the next meeting, Jonathan obviously had decided to involve himself more actively in the group process. He began by addressing another group member who had not disclosed much about her own reasons for attending the workshop. Betty looked at him and acknowledged that she had many issues similar to Jonathan's to work out. "By listening to the stories of others in this workshop I have learned that control schemes are not accidental. They have a logical structure and have to be dealt with in a planned, logical process. Coming here has been my first step. I want to learn to take control over my future and my well-being. Disclosing your struggles to us has helped me in being less critical with myself," she smiled at Jonathan.

For the first time, Jonathan's face showed a relaxed expression. He had moved from being a forced participant within his family to observer and to active participant in some parts of his life rather than remaining a victim and sitting on the sidelines. Now he experienced the good feelings that result from being acknowledged for his contribution. As small as the incident was, it marked a significant shift in his life.

As Jonathan shared with the group members, he had great difficulties practicing a more assertive stance with his family and most other people. The greatest hurdle was imagining himself acting assured and confident. Because it felt so far from the truth, he could not even convince himself to say the words or make the movements. That was one of the reasons he did not benefit from reading self-help books.

The other day the tune "Me and My Shadow" had come into his mind, and he didn't seem able to shake it. A magician friend of his had used the tune for his act, which started with having his movements projected onto the stage curtain while being accompanied by the music. After two or three more tricks, the curtain opened and his friend continued his act to completion. It was a clever opening for the act. The movements of the magician's shadow on the curtain had intrigued Jonathan. As he was thinking about it now, he was struck by the idea of projecting new behaviors that he felt unable to perform onto his own shadow. Then watching the shadow's actions in his mind, he could later imitate those behaviors that appeared appropriate as the shadow performed them. Those behaviors that did not look natural, the shadow had to continue practicing until they were acceptable. To complete the picture, Jonathan—in his imagination—made the shadow interact with Jonathan's father, other family members, and customers in the furniture store.

As an afterthought, Jonathan added that he had run into Susie, his former girlfriend. She was pleased to hear about his participation in the workshop. Jonathan hoped that they might get back together again. Overall, Jonathan's attitude had improved.

At the next group meeting Jonathan's face reflected a mixture of anger and sadness, but also determination as he took his seat. Obviously, he was eager to talk, but he waited until everyone was seated. Then, encouraged by the group members, he started with a report about finding out his brother-in-law's likely intentions. As Jonathan had learned earlier, his father's plans included the opening of a second furniture store in another part of town. This store was supposed to be managed by Jonathan's sister Annette and her husband Bert. Recently Bert had been spending time in the main store, apparently to prepare himself for the opening of the new store.

There had been several phone calls for Bert in his absence, and Jonathan had offered to take messages for Bert. Most of the calls were from businesses, not families that might be interested in buying furniture for their homes. Jonathan became curious and began to ask the callers questions, such as was there anything he could tell Bert in preparation for a return call. Not everybody gave him an answer, but from those who did he got the impression that their call was about business furniture, especially when one caller wanted Bert to know that there would be a change in the overall office floor plan.

Group member Paul inquired about Jonathan's opinion. What did Jonathan think might be going on in the business? "My first thought was that my father and Bert might have decided to turn the new store into a business furniture place," Jonathan replied. "To follow up on that thought, at the next Friday dinner meeting, just in passing I asked what line of furniture father was focusing on for the new store. Would it be mostly like the styles we carried in the main store or would it be different? In the old days I would never have considered asking my father. I was so used to waiting until he told me. Now I think, just because he does not ask questions, does not mean I cannot ask a simple innocent question."

"What was his answer?" Paul wanted to know.

"My father said that it would not be much different from what we sell at the main store. Perhaps there would be a few styles that appealed to younger people because the population in that part of town seemed to include many young people just starting out with their families." According to Jonathan's report, his father did not say anything about business furniture and, although he usually did not tell them everything, his father did not lie.

At the time, Jonathan did not dare look at Bert or Annette, hoping that they would not attach any importance to his question. Bert seemed to confirm the father's statement when he said that it was important to have an established line of furniture at hand for younger people. "They don't really know what they want; they need a lot of guidance in making their selections," Bert added. Jonathan was not sure whether Bert's remark about the young people's buying strategies was meant to make a point of agreeing with the father, to shift the attention away from any other details of Bert's plans, or a combination of both. Nevertheless, he decided to assist Bert in downplaying for the moment any of Bert's office furniture plans by confirming how important it was to guide young people in the purchase of their furniture, because they most likely were living with those purchases for many years, and it was important for them and the business that they were happy with their selection.

"I was really glad that I had started to express myself just a little more at our Friday dinners, so my question about the type of furniture did not represent blatantly different behavior" Jonathan sounded pleased about having taken the initiative to find out more about the family business.

Praising Jonathan for the way he managed his inquiries, Paul added his opinion that Bert might be secretly planning to add another aspect to the business that he would be in charge of right from the beginning and that might overshadow the current business in sales, thereby giving Bert greater power when it came time for Jonathan's father to retire.

"That's right, Bert and your sister might push you right out of the business," Betty agreed.

Jonathan admitted that he had entertained similar thoughts. In fact, in order to avoid Bert's suspicion when he gave him the message about the change in the office layout, Jonathan did not mention the word office, acting as if it might be the layout of a home. Several days later Jonathan had a chance to mention the incident to Susie. Interestingly enough, Susie knew somebody who worked for that company, and she had heard that the company was planning to move to bigger quarters in a new office building that was near completion.

"I think you should tell your father about your suspicions. It is his business and he needs to protect it" was Bob's opinion.

"That's correct, it is my father's business, and he ought to protect it. Looking at what I have observed so far, Bert's goal could be to completely take over the business at some time in the future. I am a target person standing in the way of his goal. My father could also be a target," Jonathan admitted in a sad tone of voice, but he did not know whether his father was aware of Bert's scheme, and what is worse, if he might be in agreement with Bert. Jonathan had not formulated a plan of action yet but wanted to continue collecting evidence as inconspicuously as possible and keep a record of it, which he might present to his father if and when it seemed appropriate. In the meantime, he intended to expand his knowledge of computer applications within the furniture business. In addition, he would continue to increase his personal contact with the customers, emphasizing his cabinet-making skills, in a role as consultant to the customers rather than being a repairperson in the back of the store.

The leader agreed that Jonathan had taken great steps: "Your analysis of the probable scheme helped you with identifying yourself as the target, but as you indicated, your father might also be a target." Jonathan's decision to wait with any disclosure until he knew more about his father's position was a wise one. If Jonathan's assumption was correct, that both he and his father were targets, Jonathan would have the opportunity to observe different strategies that Bert would most likely use in his attempts to control both Jonathan and his father. It should be interesting to observe the unfolding of this scenario.

Workshop participants had become comfortable with each other, as could be observed from the way they greeted each other with smiles and full eye contact. Certainly, the disclosure of personal material had brought them closer together. They had taken on a group character of respectful friendliness. Even Bob's approach had become overall less confrontational and more accepting.

At the next meeting Jonathan was eager to report on a new experience at last Friday's dinner meeting. His father had raised the issue of advertising. Past efforts in advertising for the business had been conservative. Perhaps the father was considering changes. He asked for family members' opinions. "That was a new move for him," Jonathan said. Annette and Bert seemed to favor a more aggressive approach than the business had used in the past. Bert suggested they focus on the big family holidays and encourage customers to get their new living room or dining room furniture before Christmas without worrying about the money—no down payment and monthly payments starting at a much later time, as their competitors had been advertising. Being able to show off the new furniture to their guests over the holidays would be a better incentive for the customers to buy than if it were just for their own use at any time of the year. The holidays would provide an urgency to buy and the store could also make additional money on the financing.

Group members asked what could have prompted Jonathan's father to ask for the family's opinion. Not knowing the answer, Jonathan speculated that perhaps his father wanted to see if Annette, Bert, and Jonathan were in agreement. Without commenting on Bert's statement, the father looked at Jonathan as if he expected to hear from him. This was another new behavior coming from his father, but one Jonathan was able to cope with, thanks to his changed self-concept. As calmly as he could, Jonathan expressed his opinion that the store policies were based on the customers' trust. The store had always helped the customers to get the furniture they wanted, and the store had helped them to keep it as long as they liked it—no repossessing! The father and Bert seemed surprised at Jonathan's statement. It was brief but succinct in reflecting on the business ethics historically practiced by the family. Without encouraging any further discussion, the father stated that he would think about the issue. Jonathan admitted that he was surprised about himself and the way he spoke.

"Perhaps your father had noticed a change in you when you started to make some comments at the family dinners, as you had mentioned to us," Betty tried to interpret the situation. Jonathan agreed that could be an explanation because of another unusual event at the Friday dinner.

Following the end of the advertising discussion, his father had started on another topic. A young couple had come into the store. The woman directed her companion's attention toward a larger piece of furniture, a wall unit that could accommodate an entertainment system or a bar and open shelves for books and knickknacks. While the man took a closer look at the piece, the young woman looked around the store searching for something. The father approached her in a helpfully questioning way but she asked for the young man who had talked to her on a previous occasion. Thinking that the woman might want to be helped by someone closer to her age, the father suggested calling his daughter out to assist the woman. In response, the young woman turned toward the door, saying "Oh no, please don't bother her. We will come back when the young man is available; perhaps tomorrow will be a better time." With that she left the store with her husband following closely behind her.

Looking at Bert and Jonathan in turn, the father asked if either one of them had perhaps recently served the young woman. Bert shook his head but Jonathan, after making sure that he and his father were talking about the same piece of furniture, admitted that he had been available to help the woman with her questions. Did Jonathan have any idea why the woman might not have wanted a female sales person to help her, the father asked. Before Jonathan could answer, Annette chimed in that it might have been the same woman who was in the store perhaps a week ago who didn't seem to know what she wanted. She was an example of what Bert had explained earlier; to every one of Annette's suggestions she either shrugged her shoulders or had a negative reply.

Without another question, the father, looking at Jonathan, said "we better make sure that you are available when she comes back." That was the end of the Friday night dinner conversation. For the first time in a long time, Jonathan did not feel threatened by his father. He thought that his father's behavior reflected concern rather than anger or displeasure. Jonathan disclosed his hopes that his slowly and carefully changed behavior might not have hurt him in his father's eyes. He added that Susie might change her attitude about him too, now that Jonathan had taken decisive steps toward his future. This was enough encouragement to continue with re-creating or restructuring himself and was also reason to continue with his observations and keep a record of Bert's activities. Jonathan sounded determined not to be squeezed out of his part of the family business.

Group members wanted to know if the woman ever came back into the store. Jonathan reported that the next day, a Saturday, he saw the woman outside the store window, standing next to the young man. When she caught sight of Jonathan, she waved to him and pulled the young man with her into the store. She seemed greatly relieved and explained to her husband that Jonathan had been the one who had helped her so much in deciding what would be a good purchase for their new home. She had mentioned that she liked the teakwood wall unit, although it would mean they could not buy anything else for a while. The price for the wall unit was high but she thought it was justified. She wanted to make sure that this piece of furniture would not clash with what they already had and that it would blend in with future purchases.

At her first visit to the store, Jonathan had asked her about the color schemes in the room she wanted to place the wall unit in as well as what other types of furniture she might be thinking of adding in the future. When he had her answers he brought out some pieces of wallboard and some drapery remnants from the backroom. The woman had been concerned about the color of one wall that was different from the rest of them, a kind of avocado green. How would the color of the teakwood work with that wall color and with the expensive brocade draperies her parents had given the young couple? The young woman seemed pleased and told Jonathan that she would return with her husband to get his opinion.

Now with her husband accompanying her, Jonathan, anticipating her request, brought out the materials again and in addition placed a vase and a glazed ceramic bowl that either accented or complimented the colors and the shape of the wall unit. After she looked at it, nodding her head, Jonathan placed some smaller pieces of furniture of a different style near the wall unit, demonstrating how the wall unit might form a harmonious whole with future purchases. The young woman was delighted, her husband praised her good taste, and they purchased the wall unit, along with the vase, and the ceramic bowl. While he was completing the sale, Jonathan noticed his father moving around in the back of the store.

It was the last meeting of the workshop; Jonathan was eager to tell the group that Susie had agreed to become engaged to him again. He had convinced her that his attempts to change parts of his personality were genuine. Jonathan knew he had a long way to go, but he had made a good start. He felt that his participation in the workshop had given him a new lease on life, just when he believed that he was doomed to stay forever in the backroom of the furniture store. Now he was working on getting ready to face the lights.

Observing quietly the control techniques employed by his father, his sister, and his brother-in-law had enabled him to use some of the information in asserting his opinion in a way that was outwardly not so much out of character for him that it would have drawn premature attention to his goals. Instead, he made an impression of seriously and sincerely considering value positions for the company, a position his father would most likely be in agreement with.

What about Jonathan's desire to become a comedian? Group members asked. Jonathan thought for a moment before he answered. "I still would like to give that a try. In fact, I considered taking my act to a few cities within a 300-mile radius from here. With an assumed name—it could be my shadow's name—people here would not even know about it. When I mentioned it to Susie, she understood that I wanted to try it out. On the other hand, I feel better about the furniture business now that I have taken steps to carve out a place for myself. Best of all, I don't have to look for a profession to hide behind anymore. Thanks to this group experience, I have a different outlook on my life." Jonathan was eager for the new cycle of the workshop to begin; there would be many more hurdles to confront in the process of restructuring his personality and his life.

The way Jonathan used the idea of his shadow and observing its actions could make one think of a special application of psychologist Albert Bandura's theory on social cognitive learning, discussed in Chapter 6. If the shadow's behaviors appeared appropriate without eliciting negative consequences, Jonathan could try on those behaviors for himself. One could argue that Jonathan could achieve the same results by observing other confident people and imitating their behaviors. However, taking the step from others to himself loomed too great in his mind. His shadow was closer to Jonathan than those other people and the likelihood of successfully adopting his shadow's behaviors was greater than using other models that he perceived as being basically so different from Jonathan in personality traits. If he could imagine his shadow's behaviors being reinforced by the environment, he could adopt those behaviors for himself.

Jonathan assumed the ultimate in control, the power to re-create himself according to his wishes. With that he is joining the ranks of George Sand, Madonna, and others who reserved the right for themselves to be what they wanted to be. And in the end, if we accept and respect people's right to re-create themselves, we might as well accept and respect their methods of doing so.

References

Adler, A. (1979). On the origin of the striving for superiority and of social inter-
    est. In H. L. Ansbacher & R. R. Ansbacher (Eds.) (original work published
    1933) *Superiority and social interest* (3rd rev. ed., pp. 29–40). New York: Norton.
Age-of-the-Sage. *The diplomacy of Metternich: The Congress of Vienna.* http://www.
    age-of-the-sage.org/historical/biography/metternich.html, retrieved 11/29/09.
Anderson, K. L., & Umberson, D. (2001). Gendering violence: Masculinity and
    power in men's accounts of domestic violence. *Gender & Society, 15,* 358–380.
Aronson, E. (1999). The power of self-persuasion. *American Psychologist, 54,* 875–884.
Avakame, E. F. (1998). Intergenerational transmission of violence, self-control,
    and conjugal violence: A comparative analysis of physical violence and psy-
    chological aggression. *Violence and Victims, 13,* 301–316.
Bandura, A. (1986). *Social function of thought and action: A social-cognitive theory.*
    Englewood Cliffs, NJ: Prentice-Hall.
Bartlett, J. (1968). *Familiar quotations* (14th ed. Revised and enlarged, E. M. Beck,
    Ed.) Boston: Little, Brown.
Baumeister, R. F. (1997). Esteem, threat, self-regulatory breakdown, and emo-
    tional distress as factors in self-defeating behavior. *Review of General Psychology,
    1,* 145–174.
Baumeister, R. F., Heatherton, T. F., & Tice, D. M. (1994). *Losing control: How and
    why people fail at self-regulation.* San Diego, CA: Academic Press.

Beattie, M. (1987). *Codependent no more.* (reissued with a new preface in 1992). New York: HarperCollins.

Becker, G. de (1997). *The gift of fear: Survival signals that protect us from violence.* New York: Little, Brown.

Blanton, H., & Christie, C. (2003). Deviance regulation: A theory of action and identity. *Review of General Psychology, 7,* 115–149.

Boush, D. M., Friestad, M., & Wright, P. (2009). *Deception in the marketplace: The psychology of deceptive persuasion and consumer self protection.* New York: Routledge/ Taylor & Francis Group.

Buller, D. B., & Burgoon, J. K. (1994). Deception: Strategic and non-strategic communication. In J. A. Daly & J. M. Wiemann (Eds.) *Strategic interpersonal communication* (pp. 191–224). Hillsdale, NJ: Erlbaum.

Burns, D. D. (1980, November). The perfectionist's script for self-defeat. *Psychology Today,* 34–52.

Cialdini, R. B. (1993). *Influence: Science and practice* (3rd ed.). New York: HarperCollins.

Cialdini, R. B. (2001). *Influence: Science and practice.* Boston: Allyn & Bacon.

DeLozier, M. W., & Rodrigue, J. (1996). Marketing to the homosexual (gay) market: A profile and strategy implications. In D. L. Wardlow (Ed.), *Gays, lesbians, and consumer behavior: Theory, practice, and research issues in marketing* (pp. 203–212). New York: Haworth Press.

Digman, J. M. (1990). Personality structure: Emergence of the five-factor model. *Annual Review of Psychology, 41,* 417–440.

duCoudray, H. (1936) *Metternich.* New Haven, CT: Yale University Press.

Dutton, D. G. (1995a). Male abusiveness in intimate relationships. *Clinical Psychology Review, 15,* 567–581.

Dutton, D. G. (1995b). Intimate abusiveness. *Clinical Psychology: Science and Practice, 2,* 207–224.

Dutton, D. G., Saunders, K., Starzomski, A., & Bartholomew, K. (1994). Intimacy-anger and insecure attachment as precursors of abuse in intimate relationships. *Journal of Applied Social Psychology, 24,* 1367–1386.

Eidelson, R. J., & Eidelson, J. I. (2003). Dangerous ideas: Five beliefs that propel groups toward conflict. *American Psychologist, 58,* 182–192.

Festinger, L. (1957). *A theory of cognitive dissonance.* Stanford, CA: Stanford University Press.

Fishman, P. M. (1983). The work women do. In B. Thorne, C. Kramarae, & N. Henley (Eds.), *Language, gender and society* (pp. 89–101). New York: Newbury House.

Fox, R. F. (1996). *Harvesting minds: How TV commercials control kids.* Westport, CT: Praeger.

Frey, J. N. (2000). *The key: How to write damn good fiction using the power of myth.* New York: St. Martin's Press.

Gardner, H. (2004). *Changing minds: The art and science of changing our own and other people's minds.* Boston, MA: Harvard Business School Press.

Garten, J. E. (2001). *The mind of the CEO.* New York: Basic Books.

Geller, J. (2001). *Here comes the bride: Women, weddings, and the marriage mystique.* New York: Four Walls Eight Windows.

Gelman, R., Durgin, F., & Kaufman, L. (1995). Distinguishing animates from inanimates. In D. Sperber, D. Premack, & A. Premack (Eds.), *Causality and culture* (pp. 150–184). Oxford, England: Plenum.

Goffman, E. (1967). *Interaction ritual*. Garden City, NY: Anchor Books/ Doubleday.

Goldstein, N. J., Martin, S. J., & Cialdini, R. B. (2008). *Yes! 50 scientifically proven ways to be persuasive.* New York: Free Press.

Goodrum, C., & Dalrymple, H. (1990). *Advertising in America: The first 200 years.* New York: Harry N. Abrams.

Greene, R., & Elffers, J. (1998). *The 48 laws of power.* New York: Viking.

Guerin, B. (2003). Language use as social strategy: A review and an analytic framework for the social sciences. *Review of General Psychology, 7,* 251–298.

Gula, R. (2002). *Nonsense: A handbook of logical fallacies.* Mount Jackson, VA: Axios Press.

Hamby, S. L., & Sugarman, D. B. (1999). Acts of psychological aggression against a partner and their relation to physical assault and gender. *Journal of Marriage and the Family, 61,* 959–970.

Heatherton, T. F. (2000). Having and losing control: Understanding self-regulation failure. *Psychological Science Agenda, 13,* 8–9.

Held, L. (2009). Psychoanalysis shapes consumer culture. *Monitor on Psychology, 40,* Time Capsule, 32–34.

Herzog, D. (2006). *Cunning.* Princeton, NJ: Princeton University Press.

Hewitt, P. L., & Flett G. L. (1991). Perfectionism in the self and social contexts: Conceptualization, assessment, and association with psychopathology. *Journal of Personality and Social Psychology, 60,* 456–470.

Hine, T. (1993). *The total package: The evolution and secret meaning of boxes, bottles, cans, and tubes.* New York: Little, Brown.

Hollender, M. H. (1965). Perfectionism. *Comprehensive Psychology, 6,* 94–103.

Jacobson, N., & Gottman, J. (1998). *When men batter women: New insights into ending abusive relationships.* New York: Simon & Schuster.

Janke, M. A. (2000). *Power living: Mastering the art of self-discipline.* Virginia Beach, VA: Special Operations Pub.

Johnson, M. P. (1995). Patriarchal terrorism and common couple violence: Two forms of violence against women. *Journal of Marriage and the Family, 57,* 283–294.

Karoly, P. (1999). A goal systems-self-regulatory perspective on personality, psychopathology, and change. *Review of General Psychology, 3,* 264–291.

Kaukinen, C. (2004). Status compatibility, physical violence, and emotional abuse in intimate relationships. *Journal of Marriage and Family, 66,* 452–471.

Kefir, N. (1981). Impasse/priority therapy. In R. Corsini (Ed.), *Handbook of innovative psychotherapies* (pp. 400–415). New York: Wiley.

Kennedy-Moore, E., and J. C. Watson. 2001. *Expressing emotions: Myths, realities, and therapeutic strategies.* New York: Guilford.

King, D. (2008). *Vienna 1814: How the conquerors of Napoleon made love, war, and peace at the Congress of Vienna.* New York: Random House Inc.

Kohn, A. (1986). *No contest: The case against competition.* Boston: Houghton Mifflin.

Laird, J. (1991). Enactments of power through ritual. In T. J. Goodrich (Ed.) *Women and power: Perspectives for family therapy* (pp. 123–147). New York: Norton.

Landers, A. (2002, July 26) Response to 'Living dangerously in Ohio.' *The Miami Herald*, Cancun Edition. 5B.

La Rochefoucauld, F. (1968). Reflections. In J. Bartlett. *Bartlett's familiar quotations* (14th edition). Boston: Little, Brown.

Lazarus, R. S., & Lazarus, B. N. (1994) *Passion and reason: Making sense of our emotions*. New York: Oxford University Press.

Lewis, H. G. (1996). *Silver linings: Selling to the expanding mature market*. Chicago, IL: Bonus Books.

Lieberman, D. (2000). *Get anyone to do anything and never feel powerless again*. New York: St. Martin's Press.

Living Bible, paraphrased. (1971). Wheaton, IL: Tyndale House Publishers.

Luchins, A. S., & Luchins, E. H. (1978). *Revisiting Wertheimer's seminars* (Vol. 1). Lewisburg, PA: Bucknell University Press.

Maass, V. S. (2002/2006). *Women's group therapy: Creative challenges and options*. New York: Springer.

Machiavelli, N. (1950). *The prince and the discourses* (translated by Luigi Ricci, revised by E. R. P. Vincent). New York: Carlton House.

Mahoney, M. J. (1991). *Human change processes*. New York: Basic Books.

Marken, R. S. (1992). *Mind readings: Experimental studies of purpose*. Los Angeles: MindReadings.com./ (accessed March 29, 2010)

Marken, R. S. (2002). Looking at behavior through control theory glasses. *Review of General Psychology, 6*, 260–270.

Martin, J. (2009a). Here's what to tell those who hog all the leftovers. *The Indianapolis Star*, Star Classifieds, Miss Manners, November 26, 2009, p. C9.

Martin, J. (2009b). If it's inconvenient for you, don't answer the phone. *The Indianapolis Star*, Star Classifieds, Miss Manners, August, 20, 2009, p. C8.

Masten, A. S., & Coatsworth, J. D. (1998). The development of competence in favorable and unfavorable environments. *American Psychologist, 53*, 205–220.

McDougal, D. (2001). *Privileged son: Otis Chandler and the rise and fall of the L. A. Times dynasty*. Cambridge, MA: Perseus.

McGinty, S. M. (2001). *Power talk: Using language to build authority and influence*. New York: Warner Books.

Merritt, J. (2010). Sexting and the law: lessons for youth. My View. *The Indianapolis Star*, January 15, 2010. Conversations, p. A15.

Miller, B., Williams, G. A., & Hayashi, A. M. (2004). *The 5 paths to persuasion: the art of selling your message*. New York: Warner Business Books.

Mitchell, K., & Sugar, M. (2009a). The Indianapolis Star, Star Classifieds, Annie's Mailbox, July 26, 2009, p. 32. http://www.creators.com/advice/annies-mailbox.html (accessed March 29, 2010).

Mitchell, K., & Sugar, M. (2009b). She's sick of catching bugs from sister-in-law's kids. *The Indianapolis Star*, Star Classifieds, Annie's Mailbox, November 25, 2009, p. C14.

Mitchell, K., & Sugar, M. (2009c). Controlling boyfriend is a potential abuser. *The Indianapolis Star*, Star Classifieds, Annie's Mailbox, July 28, 2009. p. C5.

Mitchell, K., & Sugar, M. (2009d). Don't take stepdaughter's bait. *The Indianapolis Star*, Star Classifieds, Annie's Mailbox, August 22, 2009, p. C11.

Mitchell, K., & Sugar, M. (2009e). Help is available for abuse victims, families. *The Indianapolis Star*, Star Classifieds, Annie's Mailbox, September, 24, 2009, p. C8.

Moretti, M. M., & Higgins, E. T. (1999). Own versus other standpoints in self-regulation: Developmental antecedents and functional consequences. *Review of General Psychology, 3*, 188–223.

Murphy, J. D. (2000). *Business is combat*. New York: Regan Books.

Myers, D. G. (2005). *Exploring psychology* (6th ed.). New York: Worth.

Norwood, R. (1985). *Women Who Love Too Much*. New York: Pocket Books, a division of Simon & Schuster.

Pacht, A. R. (1984). Reflections on perfection. *American Psychologist, 39*, 386–390.

Parrott III, L. (2000). *The control freak*. Wheaton, IL: Tyndale House.

Peters, T. J., & Waterman, Jr., R. H. (1982). *In search of excellence*. New York: Harper & Row.

Petty, R. E., & Cacioppo, J. T. (1986). *Communication and persuasion: Central and peripheral routes to attitude change*. New York: Springer Verlag.

Pistole, M. C., & Arricale, F. (2003). Understanding attachment: Beliefs about conflict. Journal of *Counseling & Development, 81*, 318–328.

Plato (1991). *The republic of Plato* (A. Bloom, Trans.). New York: Basic Books (original work published 1968).

Plotnik, R. (2002). *Introduction to psychology* (6th Ed.). Pacific Grove, CA: Wadsworth.

Pratkanis, A. R., & Aronson, E. (2001). *The age of propaganda: The everyday use and abuse of persuasion* (Rev. Ed.). New York: W. H. Freeman.

Premack, D. (1990). The infant's theory of self-propelled objects. *Cognition, 36*, 1–16.

Rhodes, D., & Rhodes, K. (1998). *Vampires*. New York: Prometheus.

Riggio, R. E. (1987). *The Charisma Quotient*. New York: Dodd, Mead & Company.

Rokita, T. (2009). Former Alanar, Inc Executives charged in massive affinity fraud case. *Indiana Secretary of State: Press Releases*. http://www.in.gov/sos/press/2009/063009.html, retrieved 7/23/09.

Rosenthal, R. (2002). Covert communication in classrooms, clinics, courtrooms, and cubicles. *American Psychologist, 57*, 839–849.

Schwartz, P., & Gibb, B. (1999) *When good companies do bad things: Responsibility and risk in an age of globalization*. New York: Wiley.

Seal, M. (2009). Madoff's world. *Vanity Fair*, No. 584, April 2009, pp. 125–135, 166–173.

Seligman, M. (1975). *Helplessness*. New York: Freeman.

Skinner, B. F. (1938). *The behavior of organisms*. New York: Appleton-Century-Crofts.

Smith, D. L. (2004). *Why we lie: The evolutionary roots of deception and the unconscious mind*. New York: St. Martin's Press.

Sorotzkin, B. (1985). The quest for perfection: Avoiding guilt or avoiding shame? *Psychotherapy, 22*, 564–571.

Stenack, R. J. (2001). *Stop controlling me!* Oakland, CA: New Harbinger.

Strong, B., DeVault, C., & Cohen, T. F. (2005). *The marriage and family experience: Intimate relationships in a changing society* (9th ed.). Belmont, CA: Thomson Learning.

Theogenis. (1968). *Elegies.* In Beck, E. M. *Bartlett's familiar quotations.* 14th ed., 215.

Thorndike, E. L. (1898). Animal intelligence: An experimental study of the associative process in animals. *Psychological Review Monograph Supplement, 2* (8).

Thorne, B., Kramarae, C., & Henley, N. (1983). *Language, gender and society.* New York: Newbury House.

Tjaden, P., & Thoennes, N. (2000). *Extent, nature, and consequences of intimate partner violence: Findings from the national violence against women survey.* Washington, DC: U.S. Department of Justice, Office of Justice Programs.

Trigg, L. (2009). Ex-pastor, sons face 10 felony counts in Sullivan. *TribStar.com,* the online edition of the Tribune-Star, Terre Haute, Indiana. http://www.tribstar.com/news/local_story_181214709.html/resources_printstory, retrieved 7/23/09.

Turner, K. (Ed.) (1993). *I dream of Madonna: Women's dreams of the goddess of pop.* San Francisco: HarperCollins.

Tweed, R. G., & Dutton, D. G. (1998). A comparison of impulsive and instrumental subgroups of batterers. *Violence and Victims, 13,* 217–230.

Valian, V. (1998). *Why so slow?* Cambridge, MA: MIT Press.

Viorst, Judith (1998). *Imperfect control: Our lifelong struggle with power and surrender.* New York: Simon & Schuster.

Wall, J. K. (2003) Tricky business: Family-run firms. *The Indianapolis Star,* August 4, 2003, C 1.

Watson, J. B. (1924) *Behaviorism.* Chicago: University of Chicago Press.

Whitney, J. O., & Packer, T. (2000). *Power plays: Shakespeare's lessons in leadership and management.* New York: Simon & Schuster.

Wikipedia (2009a). *Virginia Slims.* http://en.wikipedia.org/wiki/Virginia_Slims, retrieved 12/09/09.

Wikipedia (2009b) *Camelot (the musical).* http://en.wikipedia.org/wiki/camelot_(musical), retrieved 11/29/09.

Zimbardo, P. G., & Leippe, M. R. (1991). *The psychology of attitude change and social influence.* New York: McGraw-Hill.

Index

Abandonment, fear of, 64
Adler, A., theory of individual
    psychology, 27
Advertising, 93, 144; approach based
    on business ethics, 144–45; choice
    of words in, 106; common factors
    with politics, 93
Amway dealers, 85
Anger: "buttons," 42, 57; distracting
    function of, 42; expressions of,
    43; as sign of helplessness,
    115
Anticipation of harm, creating fear,
    30
Approach-avoidance dance, dynamics,
    70–71
Attachment style, four-category
    theory of, 24–25, 26
Attachment styles, impact on
    individuals' feelings, 25

Avoidance tendencies, due to fears,
    29–30
Awareness of being a target or victim,
    136

Behaviors, as instruments of control,
    18; ingratiating, 44–46
Beliefs, role in control situations,
    59–60
Bernays, Edward, father of public
    relations, 94–96
Bismarck's goals, 127
Brand names, aura of authority, 85;
    control with, 83–85; loyalty, 109
Business advantage, pursuit of, 89–90
Business as combat, warfare
    approach, 75–77

Chisso Corporation, incidence of
    mercury pollution, 82

Classical conditioning, principles of, 97
Codependency, as control strategy, 46
Cognitive dissonance theory, 103; experiment about, 103
Competence, belief in ability to master, 19
Competition, 30; controlling function of, 75; in sports, 31; in family businesses, 86–89; in fund raising, 89
Competitive values, in business, 78–79
Compulsions, 118–20; illusions of control, 118
Control: attempts, in infancy, 17–19; scale of, 55; behaviors, early practice, 17–18; behaviors, theoretical views, 10–11; children's struggle for, 22; competition for, 30–31; components of, 21; expectations about being in, 1; in family enterprises, 86–89, 135, 137–40, 142–44; goals and targets of, 23, 25, 26, 47, 50, 51, 132; in groups, 12–15; illusions of, obsessions, compulsions, 117–19; internal struggle for, 117–20; in intimate relationships, 61–65, 132; issues, in the courtroom, 39, 62–63; loss of, 15; obsession with, 28–29; as relationship glue, 71–74; sanctioned by society, 2; sense of being in, 16; as source of happiness, 18; strategies, used by parents, 20–21, 141; strivings, motivation for, 2, 29; tips for, 108–10; types of, 2; within the self, 15. *See also* manipulation
Control tactics from those we know, 56–57
Control techniques, 11–12; brand names and home parties, 83–85; in business, 78–81; call waiting, mobile phones, 51–52; codependency, 46; criticizing, 48–49;

disguised as love, 42–43, 115; emotional blackmail, 41–42; emotional distancing, 47; emotional vampirism, 46–47; eye contact, 39; female versions of, 68, 71–73, 134; the "helpless victim," 43; ingratiating behavior, 44–45, 98; intimidation, 63–64; irrefutable questions and statements, 60–61, 121–22, 123, 132; misguided, 52–53; physical abuse, 65–67; pushing anger buttons, 43, 57; recognizing the goals behind, 47; questions, use of, 39–40, 49–50, 120; sexting, 64; temper tantrums, 41; unspecified commitments, 48
Controllers, and their targets, 69–71, 72–74
Controlling, friends, 57–59; relationships, 69–74; through situational factors, 3
Customer, control of in business, 79–81; research about, 96

Deception, in marketing, 9–10
Deception-expectation alliance, 8–9
Deference, rules of, 36
Developmental tasks: adjustment to changes, 19; mastery and constraint, 22
Discourse, as a form of domination, 37–38
Domestic violence, 66–67

Emotional arousal, impact on decision making, 90
Emotional language, suggestive function of, 106–7
Emotionally charged issues, impact of, 90–91
Emotions, and physical violence, 65–67; leading to self-regulation breakdown, 114–17
Engagement ring, symbol of commitment, 7

Environmental directives, 3
Expectations, controlling effects of, 3, 6–8
Expectancy effects, 4–5

Fear of failure, and competition, 30–31
Frustration tolerance, under stress, 113

Gendered power, and inequality, 39
Goals behind control techniques, 47–50; discovering the, 50–52
Goals and values conflict in family enterprises, 86–89
Golden Rule, application of, 60
Groups: collective mindset, 14–15; inclusion into, 12–13

Hypnosis, as tool for control, 96

Identity, forging one's own, 130
Impulse control, ability for, 112
Influence, main elements of, 101
Interaction rituals, control systems sanctioned by society, 35–36
Intimate terrorism, 66
Intimidation, 63–64
Irrefutable statements or quewstions, 60–61, 121–22; purpose of, 123, 132

Jealousy, possessiveness, 26, 42–43, 115, 117; meaning in common language, 116

Lady Macbeth and Cleopatra, archetypes of the scheming woman, 68
Language and speech patterns, as control techniques, 37–41
Language: affect of control, 38; as form of domination, 38; interruptions, 38, 40; predictability of, 38; use of, 106; use of questions, 39–40, 49, 120

Law of effect, behaviorism, 97
Los Angeles Times, 89, 107–8
Love, as obsession, 116–17
Loyalty, on and off the job, 82
Lucky Strike's "Torches of Freedom" campaign, 95

Machiavelli, advice, 127
Manipulation, 2; parental, 141; in romantic relationships, 64–65; range of meanings, 2; web of, 1
Marken, R., control theory prescription approach, 10–11
Marketing: entitlement approach, 110; use of fear and guilt, 104, 110
Mass media, power of, 93, 107, 108
Mastery and constraint, learning of, 21–23
Mesmer, Franz Anton, magnets redirecting bodily fluids, 96
Metternich's diplomacy, 101–2

National City Lines consortium, anti-trust suit, 108
Natural tendencies, nature or nurture? 139–40

Obsessive-compulsiveness, 28, 117
Operant conditioning, 97
Order, exaggerated need for, 123–24

Packaging, 103–5, image, in politics, 105; image vs. product, 105
Parents, living vicariously through their children, 20–21
Partnership of controller and controllee, dynamics of, 69–70
Paychecks demanding loyalty, 81–83
Perfection, strivings for and control, 27–28
Perfectionism, types of, 27–28
Persistence, misinterpreted as love, 32; power of, 31; as violation of others' rights, 34

Persistent personality and control, 31–32
Personal space, concept, 11
Personality, five-factor model of, 24
Personality patterns, and control, 23–24; foundations of, 18–19, 23
Personality priorities, concept of, 19
Personality, restructuring of, 131, 135, 140, 146–48
Persuasion, 40–41, 93, 96; in business, 78; customer research on, 96–97; hypnosis, as tool of, 96; overlap with propaganda, 93–94; power of, 10; routes of approach, 100; techniques of, 98–101, 132–33
Ponzi schemes, 8, 85
Principle of consistency, in marketing, 99
Principle of scarcity, in marketing, 99
Propaganda, 94–95; facets of, 94; focus on decision-making process, 98; and public relations, 94–95
Psychological principles, as basis for control, 97–98; applied to sales pitch, 109–10
Public information, controlling transmission of, 107–8
Purpose of, 103–4

Questions, use of as verbal control, 39–40

Rituals: supporting beliefs, 37; interaction, 35, 36; legitimizing control, 3; maintaining control, 16, 138
Rosenthal, R., interpersonal expectancy effects study, 4–5
Rules of conduct, 36

Self, recreating one's, 129–31; example of, 135–48
Self-control, 15
Self-determination, 15

Self-discipline, 16, 127; from beginning to end, 127–28; power of, 126, 129
Self-fulfilling prophecies, 107
Self-handicapping, methods of, 113–14
Self-help books, and self-control, 125–26
Self-management: acts of, 124; charisma, 125; concepts, 114; techniques, 124
Self-persuasion, effectiveness of, 102–3
Self-regulation, 111–12; breakdown of, 112–14; guideline development for, 112; repair of system of, 126
Self-victimization, 2
Seligman, M., control as source of happiness, infant study, 18
Silence, as control, 38, 138; enhancing self-control effects, 128; with threatening undertones, 137
Social cognitive learning theories, 97–98; special application of, 147
Speech strategies, based in positions of inequality, 39
Superstitions and myths, 119

Target population, approaches to, 102, 109–10
Targets, justifying their position, 62; identifying them, 144; becoming victims, 139
Targets' behavior, encouraging control attempts, 123
Telephone services, used in control attempts, 52
Temper tantrums and emotional blackmail as control strategies, 42–44

Tupperware parties, 84, 99

Undisputed beliefs, determining behaviors, 59–60
Vienna Congress, 102, 141
Virginia Slim's Tennis Association Tour, 95
Vulnerability: signals of, 59–60; as target for establishing a power base, 76–77

Western Union, competition for monopoly, 90
Words: choice of, 106; and labels, power of, 107
Worksheet for targets in control situations, 136
Workshop "getting control of your life," 120–24; as arena for self-restructuring, 131–47

About the Author

VERA SONJA MAASS, PhD, is a licensed clinical psychologist, marriage and family therapist, sex therapist, mental health counselor, and co-owner of Living Skills Institute, Inc., a private practice agency. She has more than 30 years experience working in mental health agencies and in private practice. Through her work and her teaching experience as adjunct faculty at local colleges, she has become intimately acquainted with individuals' hopes, dreams, and goals as well as with their disappointments when some of these dreams were shattered and the heartaches that accompanied the realization that others had taken advantage of them.

Dr. Maass is currently serving as president of the National League of American Pen Women's Indianapolis and Indiana chapters. She is the author of five earlier books, *Counseling Single Parents: A Cognitive Behavioral Approach* (2000), *Women's Group Therapy: Creative Challenges and Options* (2002/2006), *Facing the Complexities of Women's Sexual Desire* (2007), *Lifestyle Changes: A Clinician's Guide to Common Events, Challenges, and Options* (2008), and *The Cinderella Test: Would You Really Want the Shoe to Fit?* (2009).